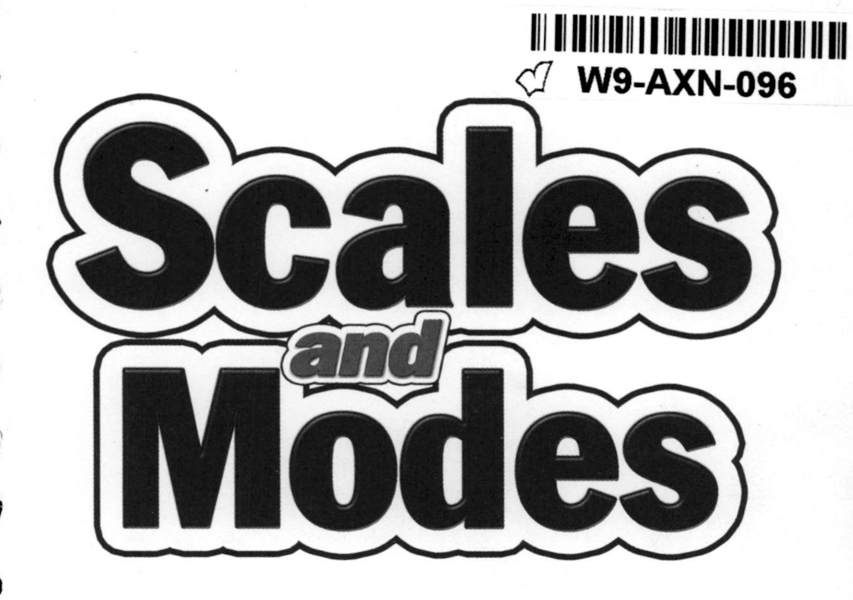


Alan Brown
& Jake Jackson

FLAME TREE
PUBLISHING

Publisher and Creative Director: Nick Wells
Project Editor: Sara Robson
Commissioning Editor: Polly Prior
Engraving: Alan Brown
Art Director: Mike Spender
Layout Design: Stephen Feather
Digital Design and Production: Chris Herbert

11 13 12
3 5 7 9 10 8 6 4

This edition first published 2009 by
FLAME TREE PUBLISHING
Crabtree Hall, Crabtree Lane
Fulham, London SW6 6TY
United Kingdom

www.flametreepublishing.com

Flame Tree Publishing is part of the Foundry Creative Media Co. Ltd



ISBN 978-1-84786-654-7

A CIP record for this book is available from the British Library
upon request.



**Alan Brown** (Engraving). A former member of the Scottish National Orchestra, Alan now works as a freelance musician, with several leading UK orchestras, and as a consultant in music and IT. Alan has had several compositions published, developed a set of music theory CD-Roms, co-written a series of Bass Guitar Examination Handbooks and worked on over 100 further titles.

Printed in China

# About This Book

**This useful new book will show you just about every scale you are likely to come across. For creative music making, either composition or improvisation, the more scales in more keys that you know the greater will be your flexibility and expressive capabilities. As an interpretative performer you will be able to understand better the music you are playing. We hope it will provide musicians of all levels with a solid point of reference that can be used to enhance music-making of all kinds.**

## The Anatomy of a Scale

Scales are invariably named after their starting note or **tonic**, also known as the **key note**, eg C in a C Major scale. It is common to number notes of a scale, with the tonic counting as one, so that we can refer to, for example, 'the fifth degree of the scale' or simply 'the fifth'. Depending on the range of your instrument, you are quite likely to be able to play higher or lower than the one-octave scales given in this book.

## Abbreviation Used in Scale Patterns

For each of the scales and modes included in this book, we have included the scale pattern. This shows the relationship between each note in the scale. For example, the scale pattern of the major scale is:

**T T S T T T S**

**S** = semitone (USA half step); **T** = tone (whole step);
**m3** = minor third (three semitones);
**a2** = augmented second (also three semitones).

# Modes

Put simply, most scales can be recycled to generate more scales with different interval structures and therefore different sounds simply by starting the new scale on each degree of the old scale. The simplest example is the set of major scale modes, which appear in several groups.

- **DORIAN:** contains the notes of the major scale starting from its **second** degree.
- **PHRYGIAN:** contains the notes of the major scale starting from its **third** degree.
- **LYDIAN:** contains the notes of the major scale starting from its **fourth** degree.
- **MIXOLYDIAN:** contains the notes of the major scale starting from its **fifth** degree.
- **AEOLIAN:** contains the notes of the major scale starting from its **sixth** degree.
- **LOCRIAN:** contains the notes of the major scale starting from its **seventh** degree.

Even though the major scale and its modal scales use the same notes, because they have different keynotes they do not have the same tonality. For example, while the major scale has a major third interval from the root to the third note and a major seventh interval from the root to the seventh note, in contrast, the Dorian modal scale has a flattened third interval from the root to the third note and a flattened seventh interval from the root to the seventh note, making it a type of minor scale.

# Using Modes

Modal scales can be used for improvising and composing melodies. Two different approaches can be taken with regard to them:

- Advanced players sometimes use modal scales as chord scales (using a different mode over each chord).
- Modes can be treated as key centres in their own right, with a group of chords to accompany each modal scale. For example, the D Dorian modal scale (see below) could be used over a D Dorian minor key centre containing any of the following chords: Dm, Em, F, G, Am, C.

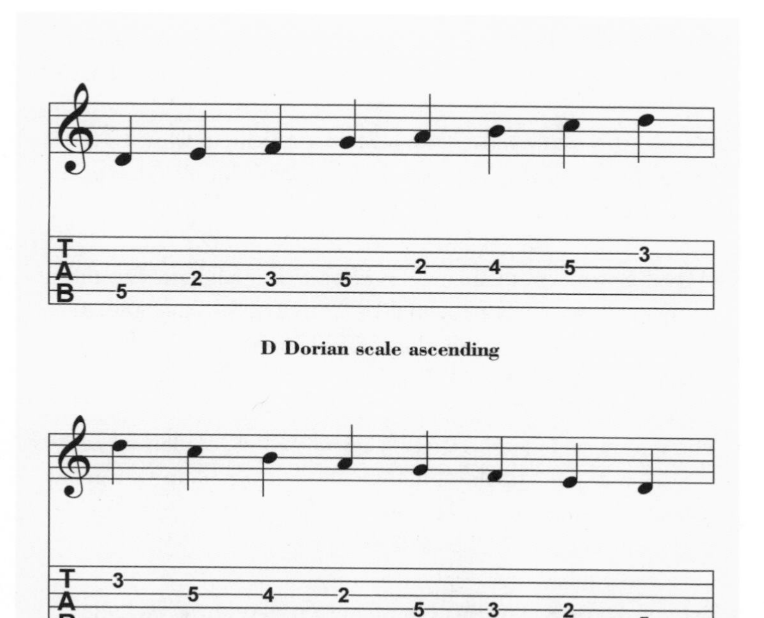


D Dorian scale ascending

D Dorian scale descending

# Scales and Modes

This book contains 31 of the most useful scales and modes, and there is one example of each for each of the 12 chromatic tones. We have divided the scales and modes included into four groups (Major, Minor, Dominant and Unusual), and for each have given a short description of how they are formed and in what style of music they might best be used.

## THE MAJOR GROUP

The third degree is important in giving a scale its basic flavour and all scales in this group have a third (four semitones, e.g. C to E) and usually a major seventh (11 semitones, e.g. C to B). Some other scales with major thirds also have minor sevenths (10 semitones, e.g. C to B♭) and appear in the Dominant Group.

- **Major:** this is the most commonly used scale in western music, being the 'Doh, Re, Mi' scale used in *The Sound Of Music*.
  **Scale Pattern: T T S T T T S**

- **Major Pentatonic:** this is a major scale with gaps (no fourth or seventh) and can be heard in many traditional tunes from places as far apart as Scotland and China.
  **Scale Pattern: T T m3 T m3**

- The major scale gives rise to a set of modes, explained earlier in the book. One of these modes, the **Lydian**, is in this group. It resembles a major scale except for the raised fourth degree.
  **Scale Pattern: T T T S T T S**

- **Lydian Augmented:** this is a modal version of the melodic minor (starting on its parent scale's third step) and is essentially a lydian with a raised, or augmented, fifth. Like all scales with an altered fifth it is restless and used in modern jazz.
  **Scale Pattern: T T T T S T S**

## THE MINOR GROUP

Here we are looking at a group of scales with minor thirds, which includes the scales commonly thought of as minor, several modal scales and a few unusual ones.

- **Natural Minor/Aeolian Mode:** this takes a major scale and starts on its sixth degree. Many folk and traditional tunes use this scale; significant notes are the flat six and seventh.
  **Scale Pattern: T S T T S T T**

- **Harmonic Minor:** this is identical to the natural minor except for the seventh degree, which is a semitone higher to make a major dominant chord possible, essential for most progressions in minor keys.
  **Scale Pattern: T S T T S a2 S**

- **Melodic Minor:** this is traditionally played with major sixth and seventh on the way up and lowered sixth and seventh on the way down. Improvising players often abandon the descending version and use exclusively the ascending form, which is consequently also called the Jazz Melodic Minor.
  **Scale Pattern: T S T T T T S** (ascending form)

- **Dorian:** This is another important modal scale, also heard in jazz but in many folk songs too. Notice that it has a major sixth but a minor seventh.
  **Scale Pattern: T S T T T S T**

- **Minor Pentatonic:** is another variant, which could be thought of as a simplified minor scale with gaps. Like the major pentatonic, it is often found in folk-melodies but also a favourite with rock guitarists.
  **Scale Pattern: m3 T T m3 T**

- **Blues:** this is created by adding one chromatic note (a raised fourth or a flattened fifth) to the minor pentatonic scale. The blues scale can also be played over a dominant seventh chord.
**Scale Pattern: m3 T S S m3 T**

- **Phrygian:** this is another scale sometimes heard in jazz or folk music. It is identical to the aeolian/natural minor except for its lowered second step.
**Scale Pattern: S T T T S T T**

- **Locrian:** this takes the notes of the phrygian and lowers its fifth step which gives an unstable brooding quality to any music using it.
**Scale Pattern: S T T S T T T**

- **Half Diminished:** if we raise the second degree of the locrian we create this scale, which is also a mode of the melodic minor.
**Scale Pattern: T S T S T T T**

## DOMINANT GROUP

The essential characteristics of dominant-type scales are the major third and minor (lowered) seventh.

- **Mixolydian:** this is the most obvious example of a dominant type scale, being simply a major scale starting on its fifth degree. You can also think of it as a major scale with a flattened seventh. Used in blues, rock, jazz and folk music.
**Scale Pattern: T T S T T S T**

- **Phrygian Major/Spanish Gypsy:** this scale starts on the fifth degree of the harmonic minor scale. Its features are the lowered second and seventh notes and it works well over a dominant chord with a flattened ninth. It is commonly used in flamenco and heavy metal music.
**Scale Pattern: S a2 S T S T T**

- **Lydian Dominant:** this is a mode of the melodic minor and has the sharp fourth of a lydian and the flat seventh of a mixolydian. Used mainly in jazz.
  **Scale Pattern: T T T S T S T**

- **Diminished Wholetone/Super Locrian/Altered:** this is also a melodic minor mode, one that starts on its seventh step. Although the third is minor, usually the lowered fourth (identical to a major third) is used to make the essential notes for a dominant chord available. Used mainly in jazz.
  **Scale Pattern: S T S T T T T**

- **Diminished/Octatonic:** this is created by adding the two altered ninths from the previous scale to the lydian dominant. It has nine different notes and can only be transposed a couple of times before it starts to repeat the same notes. Used mainly in jazz.
  **Scale Pattern: S T S T S T S T**

## UNUSUAL SCALES

Most of these scales are used less than some of the earlier ones but may prove of interest in creating more experimental sounds.

- **Chromatic:** this can be used in conjunction with any chord. As it contains all twelve semitones it can't be transposed or turned into a mode without stubbornly remaining itself.

- **Wholetone:** this also defies much transposition: if you took out every alternate note of the chromatic it would make one of the wholetone scales, the notes left making up the other. It will fit a dominant chord but with a little modification can give rise to a further set of modes (see below).
  **Scale Pattern: T T T T T T**

- **Neapolitan:** this a wholetone scale that starts and finishes with a semitone; it is also a melodic minor with a flattened second. Used, like its modes below, mainly in jazz and experimental music.
**Scale Pattern: S T T T T T S**

*The following six scales are modes of the Neapolitan scale, and are used in experimental and jazz music.*

- ***Leading Wholetone*****:** this is the second mode of the Neapolitan, as the name suggests, and is a wholetone with the extra semitone at the top.
**Scale pattern: T T T T T S S**

- ***Lydian Augmented Dominant*****:** the third mode of the Neapolitan scale is a wholetone scale with a major sixth.
**Scale pattern: T T T T S S T**

- ***Lydian Dominant* ♭6:** this is the fourth mode of the Neapolitan scale and is another wholetone with a perfect fifth available.
**Scale pattern: T T T S S T T**

- ***Major Locrian/Arabian*****:** the fifth mode of the Neapolitan scale, this is a mixolydian with flat five and six.
**Scale pattern: T T S S T T T**

- ***Semi-Locrian* ♭4:** this is the sixth mode of the Neapolitan scale, and is a wholetone scale with an added minor third.
**Scale pattern: T S S T T T T**

- ***Super Locrian* 𝄫3:** this is the seventh and final mode of the Neapolitan. It is more simply thought of as another wholetone with a semitone between the first and second degrees.
**Scale pattern: S S T T T T T**

- There is also a set of so-called **Bebop scales**, which are simply more familiar scales with an additional chromatic note. Bebop scales are frequently used in jazz improvisation. Really any scale can be embellished with a chromatic passing note, but here are a few examples.

  - ***Bebop Dominant*:** this is a mixolydian with a chromatic major seventh; use as a mixolydian.
    **Scale pattern: T T S T T S S S**

  - ***Bebop Major*:** this has the chromatic passing note between the fifth and sixth degrees.
    **Scale pattern: T T S T T S S T S**

  - ***Bebop Dorian*:** this is identical to the regular dorian with a chromatic major third between the third and fourth steps.
    **Scale pattern: T S S T T S T**

- In addition, you can always place chromatic notes in other locations (such as between fourth and fifth degrees like a blues scale) and also try turning the bebop scales into modes.

- **Byzantine/Arabic/Double Harmonic Major:** this scale has two augmented seconds. It is an exotic-sounding scale, and is sometimes used in heavy metal or flamenco music. The fourth mode of the Byzantine scale is known as the Hungarian gypsy scale.
  **Scale pattern: S a2 S T S a2 S**

**A Byzantine/Arabic/Double Harmonic Major scale ascending**

A
B♭/A♯
B
C
C♯/D♭
D
E♭/D♯
E
F
F♯/G♭
G
A♭/G♯

# A Major

**Scale pattern**

A B C♯ D E F♯ G♯ A
A G♯ F♯ E D C♯ B A

B♭/A♯
B
C
C♯/D♭
D
E♭/D♯
E
F
F♯/G♭
G
A♭/G♯

# A Major Pentatonic

**Scale pattern**

A B C♯ E F♯ A
A F♯ E C♯ B A

# A Lydian

**Scale pattern**

A B C♯ D♯ E F♯ G♯ A
A G♯ F♯ E D♯ C♯ B A

| Scale pattern | A B C♯ D♯ E♯ F♯ G♯ A<br>A G♯ F♯ E♯ D♯ C♯ B A |
|---|---|

# A Natural Minor

**Scale pattern**

A B C D E F G A
A G F E D C B A

# A Harmonic Minor

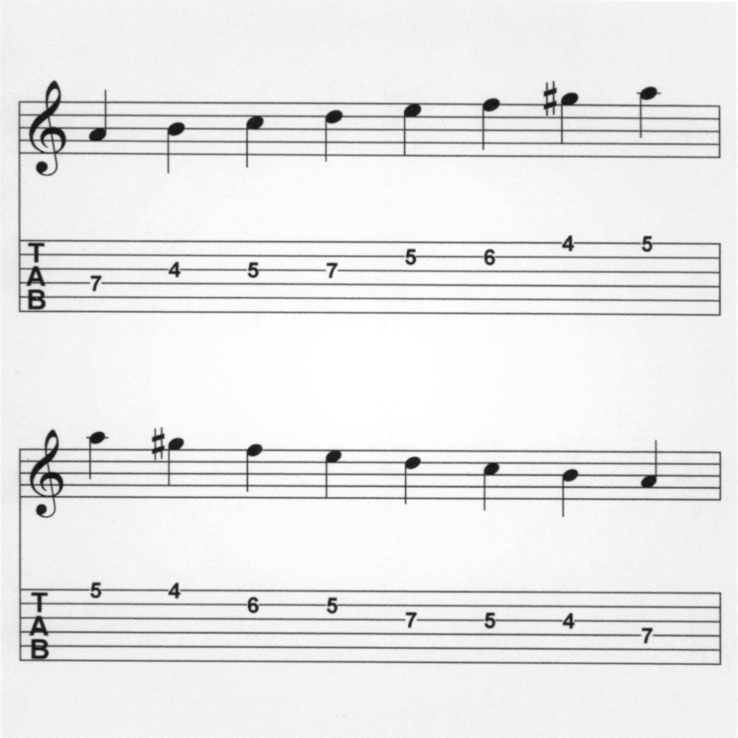

T
A
B
7 4 5 7 5 6 4 5

T
A
B
5 4 6 5 7 5 4 7

**Scale pattern**

A B C D E F G♯ A
A G♯ F E D C B A

# A Melodic Minor

| **Scale pattern** | A B C D E F♯ G♯ A<br>A G♮ F♮ E D C B A |
|---|---|

# A Dorian

TAB

2 4 5 3 5 2 3 5

TAB

5 3 2 5 3 5 4 2

**Scale pattern**

A B C D E F♯ G A
A G F♯ E D C B A

# A Minor Pentatonic

| **Scale pattern** | A C D E G A<br>A G E D C A |
|---|---|

# A Blues

B♭/A♯
B
C
C♯/D♭
D
E♭/D♯
E
F
F♯/G♭
G
A♭/G♯

TAB: 2 5 3 4 5 3 5

TAB: 5 3 5 4 3 5 2

| **Scale pattern** | A C D E♭ E♮ G A<br>A G E♮ E♭ D C A |
|---|---|

# A Phrygian

**Scale pattern**

A B♭ C D E F G A
A G F E D C B♭ A

**Scale pattern**

A B♭ C D E♭ F G A
A G F E♭ D C B♭ A

A
B♭/A♯
B
C
C♯/D♭
D
E♭/D♯
E
F
F♯/G♭
G
A♭/G♯

# A Half Diminished

**Scale pattern**

A B C D E♭ F G A
A G F E♭ D C B A

# A Mixolydian

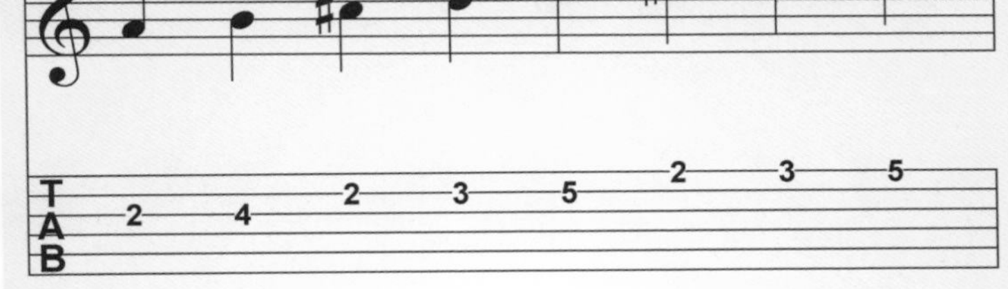

**Scale pattern**

A B C♯ D E F♯ G A
A G F♯ E D C♯ B A

# A Phrygian Major/ Spanish Gypsy

T
A
B
2 3 2 3 0 1 3 5

**Scale pattern**

A B♭ C♯ D E F G A
A G F E D C♯ B♭ A

# A Lydian Dominant

| Scale pattern | A B C♯ D♯ E F♯ G A<br>A G F♯ E D♯ C♯ B A |
|---|---|

A
B♭/A♯
B
C
C♯/D♭
D
E♭/D♯
E
F
F♯/G♭
G
A♭/G♯

# A Diminished Wholetone/ Super Locrian/Altered

**Scale pattern**

A B♭ C D♭ E♭ F G A
A G F E♭ D♭ C B♭ A

# A Diminished

**Scale pattern**

A B♭ C D♭ E♭ E♮ F♯ G A
A G F♯ E E♭ D♭ C B♭ A

A
B♭/A♯
B
C
C♯/D♭
D
E♭/D♯
E
F
F♯/G♭
G
A♭/G♯

# A Chromatic

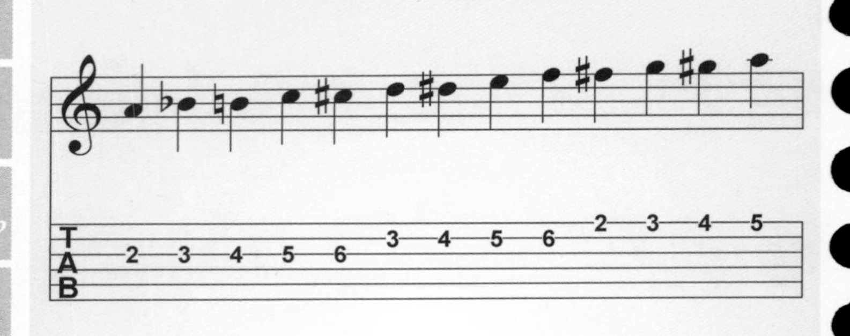

**Scale pattern**

A B♭ B♮ C C♯ D D♯ E F F♯ G G♯ A
A G♯ G♮ F♯ F♮ E D♯ D♮ C♯ C♮ B B♭ A

# A Wholetone

**Scale pattern**

A B C♯ D♯ F G A
A G F D♯ C♯ B A

A
B♭/A♯
B
C
C♯/D♭
D
E♭/D♯
E
F
F♯/G♭
G
A♭/G♯

# A Neapolitan

**Scale pattern**

A B♭ C D E F♯ G♯ A
A G♯ F♯ E D C B♭ A

# A Leading Wholetone

**Scale pattern**

A B C♯ D♯ F G G♯ A
A G♯ G♮ F D♯ C♯ B A

# A Lydian Augmented Dominant

**Scale pattern**

A B C♯ D♯ E♯ F♯ G A

A G F♯ E♯ D♯ C♯ B A

# A Lydian Dominant ♭6

**Scale pattern**

A B C♯ D♯ E F G A
A G F E D♯ C♯ B A

# A Major Locrian/Arabian

| **Scale pattern** | A B C♯ D E♭ F G A<br>A G F E♭ D C♯ B A |
|---|---|

# A Semi-Locrian ♭4

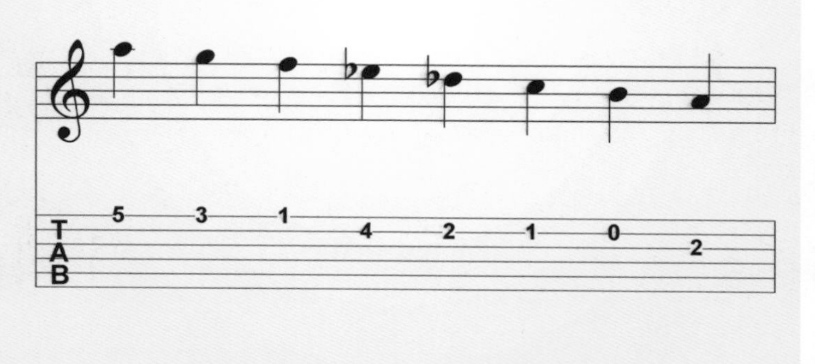


| **Scale pattern** | A B C D♭ E♭ F G A<br>A G F E♭ D♭ C B A |
|---|---|

# A Super-Locrian 𝄫3

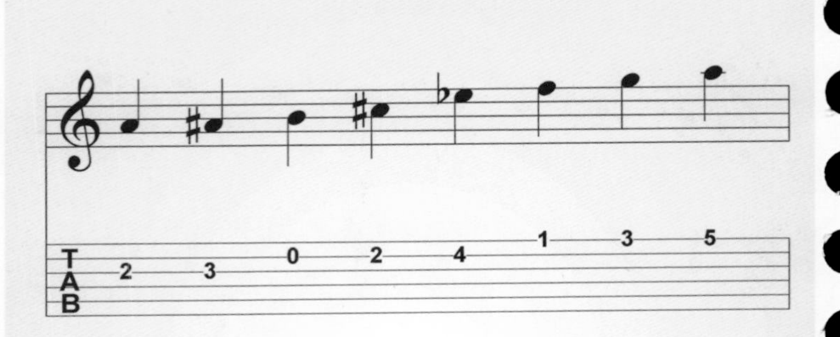


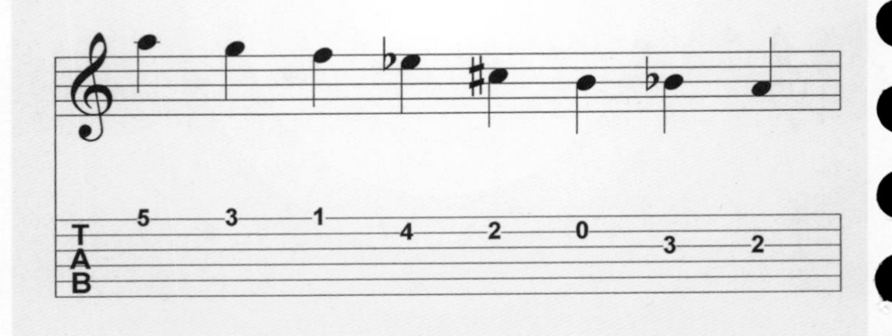


**Scale pattern**

A A♯ B C♯ E♭ F G A
A G F E♭ C♯ B B♭ A

# A Bebop Dominant

| **Scale pattern** | A B C♯ D E F♯ G G♯ A<br>A G♯ G♮ F♯ E D C♯ B A |
|---|---|

# A Bebop Major

**Scale pattern**

A B C♯ D E F♮ F♯ G♯ A
A G♯ F♯ F♮ E D C♯ B A

# A Bebop Dorian

| **Scale pattern** | A B C C♯ D E F♯ G A<br>A G F♯ E D C♯ C♮ B A |
|---|---|

A
B♭/A♯
B
C
C♯/D♭
D
E♭/D♯
E
F
F♯/G♭
G
A♭/G♯

# A Byzantine/Arabic/ Double Harmonic Major

**Scale pattern**

A B♭ C# D E F G# A
A G# F E D C# B♭ A

# B♭ Major

**Scale pattern**

B♭ C D E♭ F G A B♭
B♭ A G F E♭ D C B♭

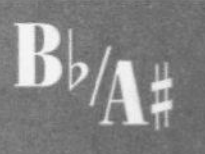

# B♭ Major Pentatonic

**Scale pattern**

B♭ C D F G B♭

B♭ G F D C B♭

# B♭ Lydian

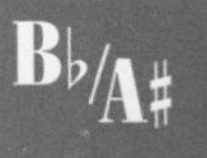


B
C
C#/D♭
D
E♭/D#
E
F
F#/G♭
G
A♭/G#

TAB
3 5 3 5 6 3 5 6

TAB
6 5 3 6 5 3 5 3

| Scale pattern | B♭ C D E F G A B♭ <br> B♭ A G F E D C B♭ |
|---|---|

# B♭ Lydian Augmented

| Scale pattern | B♭ C D E F♯ G A B♭<br>B♭ A G F♯ E D C B♭ |
|---|---|

# B♭ Natural Minor

**Scale pattern**

B♭ C D♭ E♭ F G♭ A♭ B♭

B♭ A♭ G♭ F E♭ D♭ C B♭


A
B
C
C♯/D♭
D
E♭/D♯
E
F
F♯/G♭
G
A♭/G♯

# B♭ Harmonic Minor

**Scale pattern**

B♭ C D♭ E♭ F G♭ A B♭
B♭ A G♭ F E♭ D♭ C B♭

# B♭ Melodic Minor

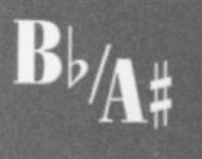


B
C
C#/D♭
D
E♭/D#
E
F
F#/G♭
G
A♭/G#

**Scale pattern**

B♭ C D♭ E♭ F G A B♭
B♭ A♭ G♭ F E♭ D♭ C B♭

# B♭ Dorian

| Scale pattern | B♭ C D♭ E♭ F G A♭ B♭<br>B♭ A♭ G F E♭ D♭ C B♭ |
|---|---|

# B♭ Minor Pentatonic

| **Scale pattern** | B♭ D♭ E♭ F A♭ B♭<br>B♭ A♭ F E♭ D♭ B♭ |
|---|---|

A
B♭/A♯
B
C
C♯/D♭
D
E♭/D♯
E
F
F♯/G♭
G
A♭/G♯

# B♭ Blues

**Scale pattern**

B♭ D♭ E♭ F♭ F♮ A♭ B♭
B♭ A♭ F♮ F♭ E♭ D♭ B♭

# A♯ Phrygian

| Scale pattern | A♯ B C♯ D♯ E♯ F♯ G♯ A♯<br>A♯ G♯ F♯ E♯ D♯ C♯ B A♯ |
|---|---|

# A♯ Locrian

**Scale pattern**

A♯ B C♯ D♯ E F♯ G♯ A♯
A♯ G♯ F♯ E D♯ C♯ B A♯

# A♯ Half Diminished

| **Scale pattern** | A♯ B♯ C♯ D♯ E F♯ G♯ A♯<br>A♯ G♯ F♯ E D♯ C♯ B♯ A♯ |
|---|---|

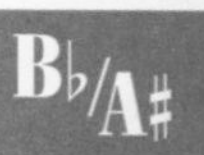
B
C
C♯/D♭
D
E♭/D♯
E
F
F♯/G♭
G
A♭/G♯

# B♭ Mixolydian

**Scale pattern**

B♭ C D E♭ F G A♭ B♭

B♭ A♭ G F E♭ D C B♭

# B♭ Phrygian Major/ Spanish Gypsy

T
A
B
3 4 3 4 1 2 4 6

**Scale pattern**

B♭ C♭ D E♭ F G♭ A♭ B♭
B♭ A♭ G♭ F E♭ D C♭ B♭

A
B♭/A#
B
C
C#/D♭
D
E♭/D#
E
F
F#/G♭
G
A♭/G#

# B♭ Lydian Dominant

**Scale pattern**

B♭ C D E F G A♭ B♭
B♭ A♭ G F E D C B♭

# A♯ Diminished Wholetone/ Super Locrian/Altered

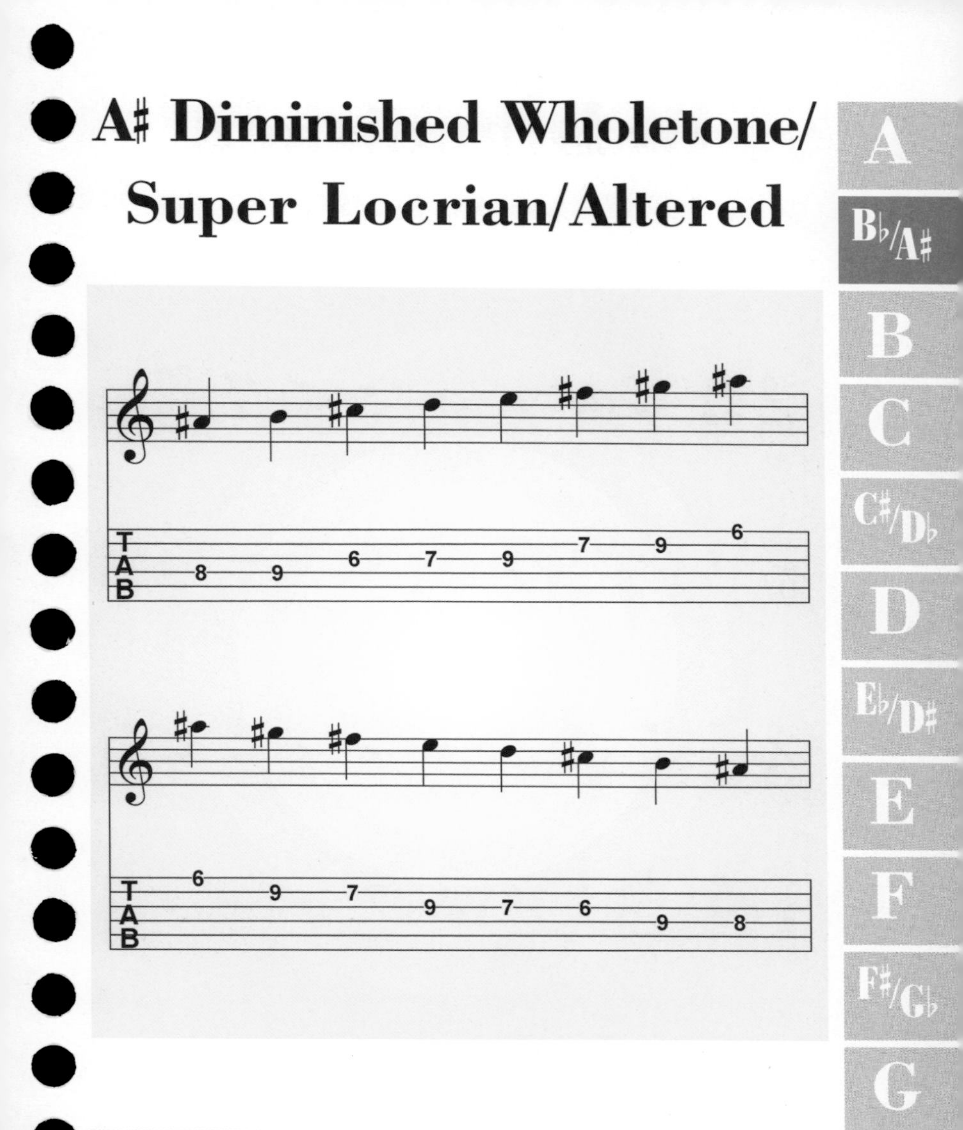


**Scale pattern**

A♯ B C♯ D E F♯ G♯ A♯
A♯ G♯ F♯ E D C♯ B A♯

# B♭ Diminished

**Scale pattern**

B♭ C♭ D♭ D♮ E F G A♭ B♭

B♭ A♭ G F E D♮ D♭ C♭ B♭

# B♭ Chromatic

**Scale pattern** B♭ C♭ C♮ D♭ D♮ E♭ E♮ F G♭ G♮ A♭ A♮ B♭
B♭ A A♭ G G♭ F E E♭ D D♭ C C♭ B♭

A
B♭/A♯
B
C
C♯/D♭
D
E♭/D♯
E
F
F♯/G♭
G
A♭/G♯

# B♭ Wholetone

| **Scale pattern** | B♭ C D E G♭ A♭ B♭<br>B♭ A♭ G♭ E D C B♭ |
|---|---|

# B♭ Neapolitan

**Scale pattern**

B♭ C♭ D♭ E♭ F G A B♭
B♭ A G F E♭ D♭ C♭ B♭

# B♭ Leading Wholetone

**Scale pattern**

B♭ C D E F♯ G♯ A B♭

B♭ A G♯ F♯ E D C B♭

# B♭ Lydian Augmented Dominant

T
A
B
3 1 3 0 2 3 4 6

**Scale pattern**

B♭ C D E F♯ G A♭ B♭
B♭ A♭ G F♯ E D C B♭

A
B♭/A♯
B
C
C♯/D♭
D
E♭/D♯
E
F
F♯/G♭
G
A♭/G♯

# B♭ Lydian Dominant ♭6

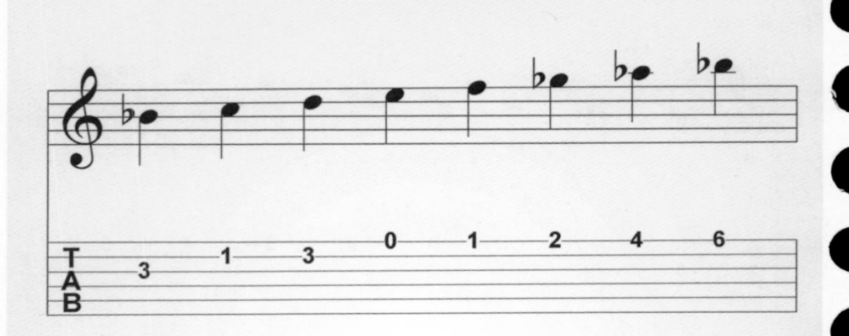

**Scale pattern**

B♭ C D E F G♭ A♭ B♭

B♭ A♭ G♭ F E D C B♭

# B♭ Major Locrian/Arabian

| **Scale pattern** | B♭ C D E♭ F♭ G♭ A♭ B♭ |
|---|---|
| | B♭ A♭ G♭ F♭ E♭ D C B♭ |

# B♭ Semi-Locrian ♭4

**Scale pattern**

B♭ C C♯ D E F♯ A♭ B♭
B♭ A♭ F♯ E D D♭ C B♭

# A♯ Super-Locrian 𝄫3

| Scale pattern | A♯ B C D E F♯ G♯ A♯<br>A♯ G♯ F♯ E D C B A♯ |
| --- | --- |

# B♭ Bebop Dominant

**Scale pattern**

B♭ C D E♭ F G A♭ A♮ B♭

B♭ A A♭ G F E♭ D C B♭

# B♭ Bebop Major

**Scale pattern**

B♭ C D E♭ F G♭ G♮ A B♭

B♭ A G♮ G♭ F E♭ D C B♭

# B♭ Bebop Dorian

**Scale pattern**

B♭ C D♭ D♮ E♭ F G A♭ B♭
B♭ A♭ G F E♭ D D♭ C B♭

# B♭ Byzantine/Arabic/ Double Harmonic Major

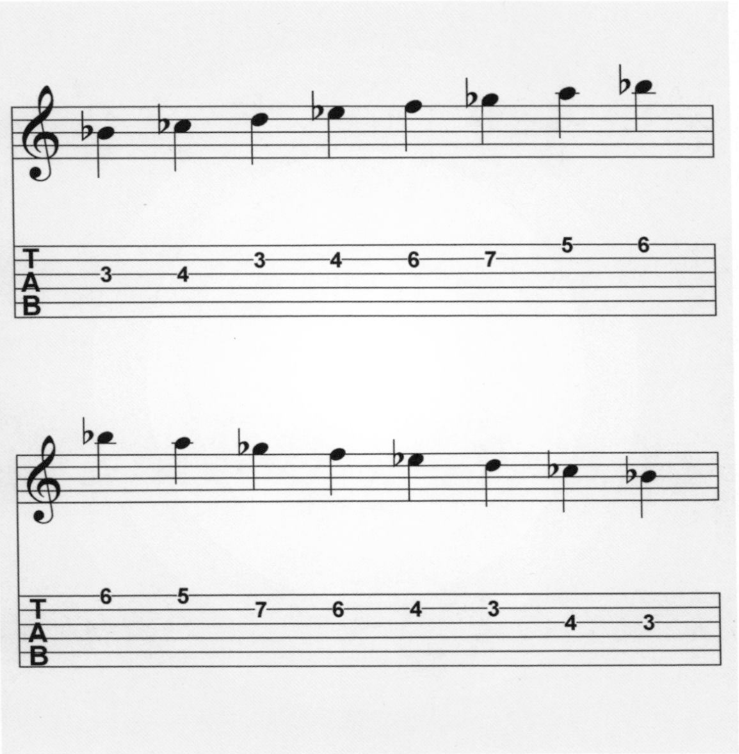

T
A
B
3 4 3 4 6 7 5 6

T
A
B
6 5 7 6 4 3 4 3

| **Scale pattern** | B♭ C♭ D E♭ F G♭ A B♭ |
| --- | --- |
| | B♭ A G♭ F E♭ D C♭ B♭ |

# B Major

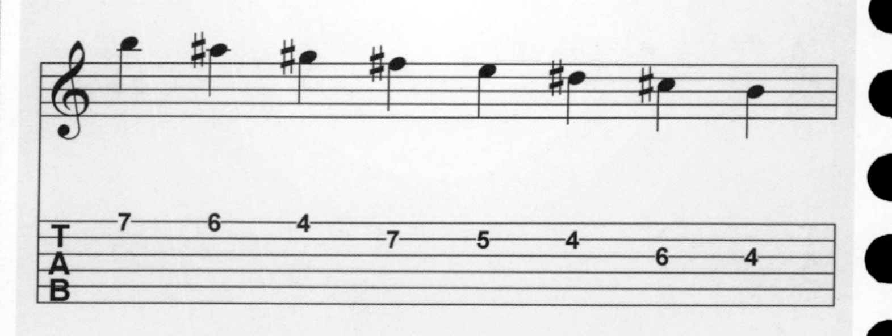


**Scale pattern**

B C♯ D♯ E F♯ G♯ A♯ B
B A♯ G♯ F♯ E D♯ C♯ B

# B Major Pentatonic

**Scale pattern**

B C♯ D♯ F♯ G♯ B
B G♯ F♯ D♯ C♯ B

A
B♭/A#
B
C
C#/D♭
D
E♭/D#
E
F
F#/G♭
G
A♭/G#

# B Lydian

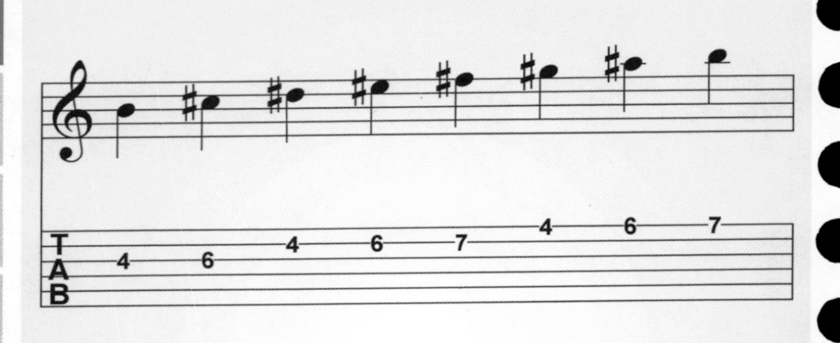

**Scale pattern**

B C# D# E# F# G# A# B

B A# G# F# E# D# C# B

| Scale pattern | B C♯ D♯ E♯ Fx G♯ A♯ B<br>B A♯ G♯ F× E♯ D♯ C♯ B |
| --- | --- |

# B Natural Minor

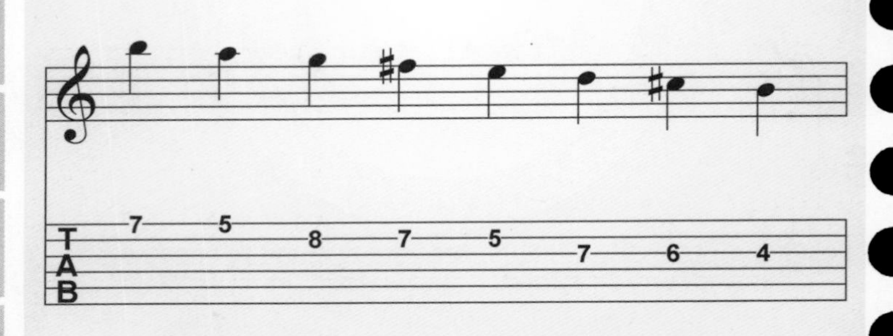


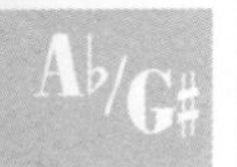


**Scale pattern**

B C♯ D E F♯ G A B
B A G F♯ E D C♯ B

# B Harmonic Minor

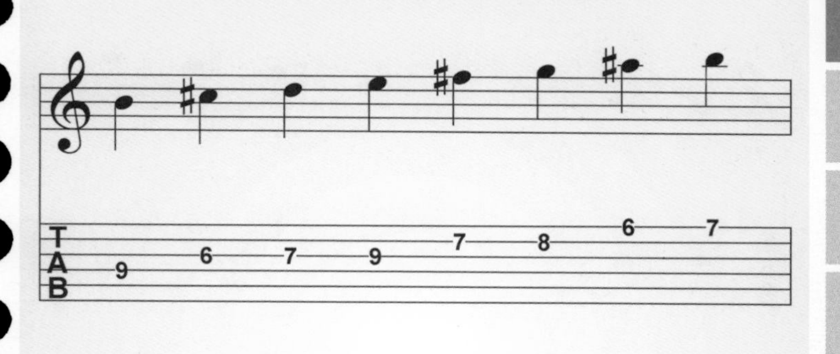

| **Scale pattern** | B C♯ D E F♯ G A♯ B<br>B A♯ G F♯ E D C♯ B |
|---|---|

A
B♭/A♯
B
C
C♯/D♭
D
E♭/D♯
E
F
F♯/G♭
G
A♭/G♯

# B Melodic Minor

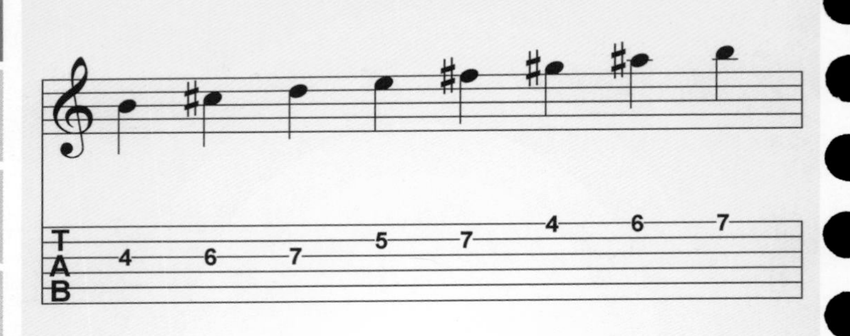

**Scale pattern**

B C♯ D E F♯ G♯ A♯ B
B A♮ G♮ F♯ E D C♯ B

# B Dorian

**Scale pattern**

B C♯ D E F♯ G♯ A B
B A G♯ F♯ E D C♯ B

# B Minor Pentatonic

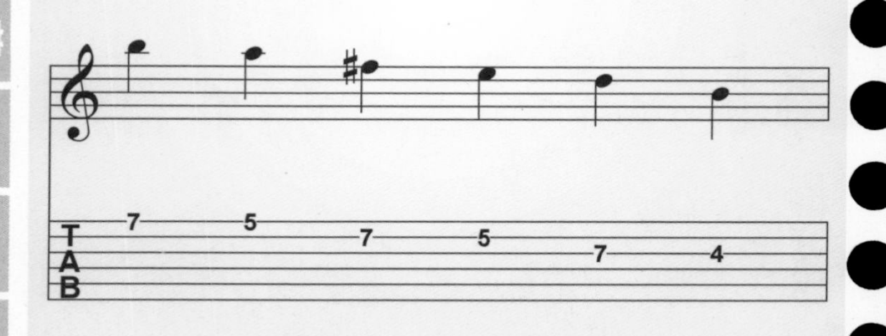


| **Scale pattern** | B D E F♯ A B<br>B A F♯ E D B |
|---|---|

# B Blues

T
A
B
4 7 5 6 7 5 7

**Scale pattern**

B D E F♮ F♯ A B
B A F♯ F♮ E D B

# B Phrygian

**Scale pattern**

B C D E F♯ G A B
B A G F♯ E D C B

# B Locrian

| **Scale pattern** | B C D E F G A B<br>B A G F E D C B |
|---|---|

A
B♭/A♯
B
C
C♯/D♭
D
E♭/D♯
E
F
F♯/G♭
G
A♭/G♯

# B Half Diminished

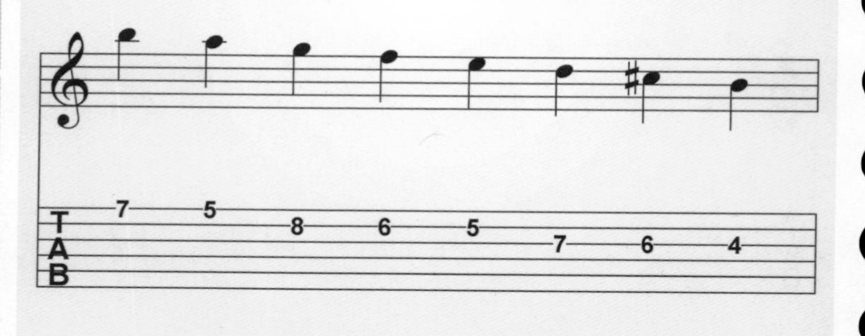


**Scale pattern**

B C♯ D E F G A B
B A G F E D C♯ B

# B Mixolydian

T
A
B
4 6 4 5 7 4 5 7

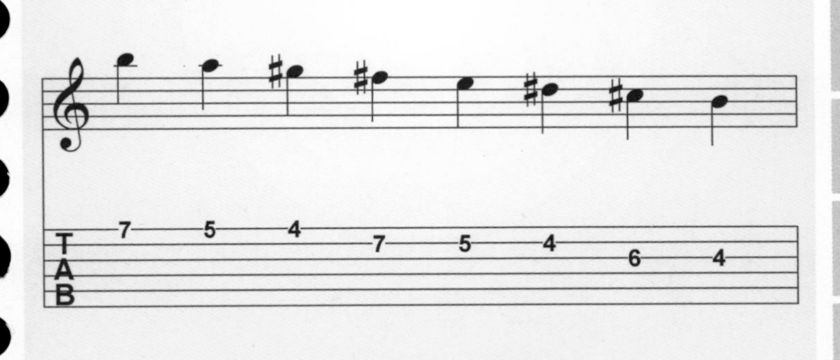


**Scale pattern**

B C♯ D♯ E F♯ G♯ A B
B A G♯ F♯ E D♯ C♯ B

A
B♭/A♯
B
C
C♯/D♭
D
E♭/D♯
E
F
F♯/G♭
G
A♭/G♯

A
B♭/A♯
B
C
C♯/D♭
D
E♭/D♯
E
F
F♯/G♭
G
A♭/G♯

# B Phrygian Major/ Spanish Gypsy

T
A
B
0 1 4 0 2 3 5 7

| **Scale pattern** | B C D♯ E F♯ G A B<br>B A G F♯ E D♯ C B |
|---|---|

# B Lydian Dominant

| Scale pattern | B C♯ D♯ E♯ F♯ G♯ A B<br>B A G♯ F♯ E♯ D♯ C♯ B |
|---|---|

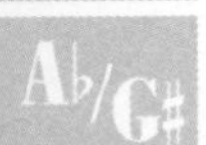


# B Diminished Wholetone/ Super Locrian/Altered

| **Scale pattern** | B C D E♭ F G A B<br>B A G F E♭ D C B |
|---|---|

# B Diminished

| **Scale pattern** | B C D E♭ F F♯ G♯ A B<br>B A G♯ F♯ F♮ E♭ D C B |
|---|---|

A
B♭/A♯
B
C
C♯/D♭
D
E♭/D♯
E
F
F♯/G♭
G
A♭/G♯

# B Chromatic

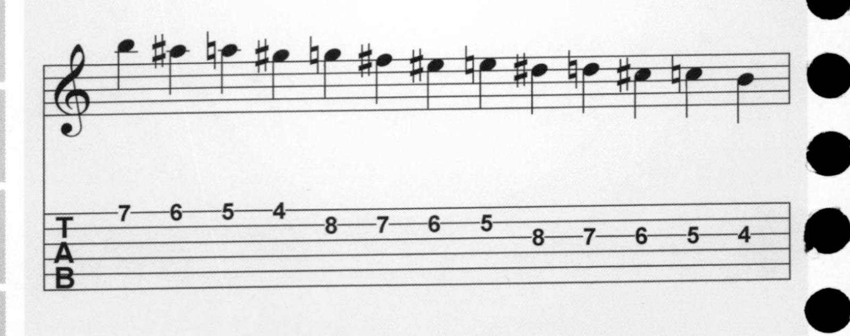


**Scale pattern**

B C C♯ D D♯ E E♯ F♯ G G♯ A A♯ B

B A♯ A♮ G♯ G♮ F♯ E♯ E♮ D♯ D♮ C♯ C♮ B

# B Wholetone

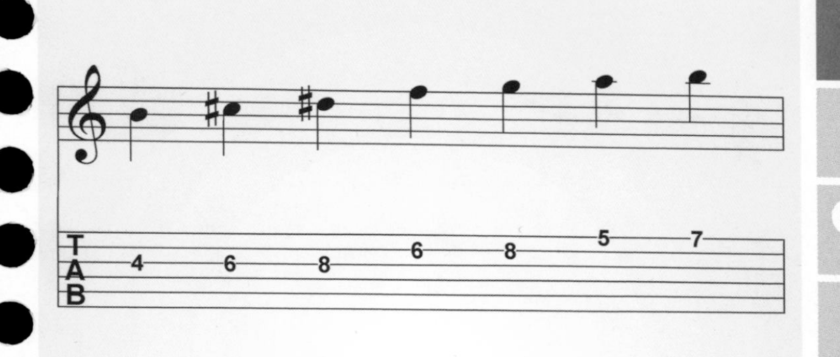

| **Scale pattern** | B C♯ D♯ F G A B<br>B A G F D♯ C♯ B |
|---|---|

A
Bb/A#
B
C
C#/Db
D
Eb/D#
E
F
F#/Gb
G
Ab/G#

# B Neapolitan

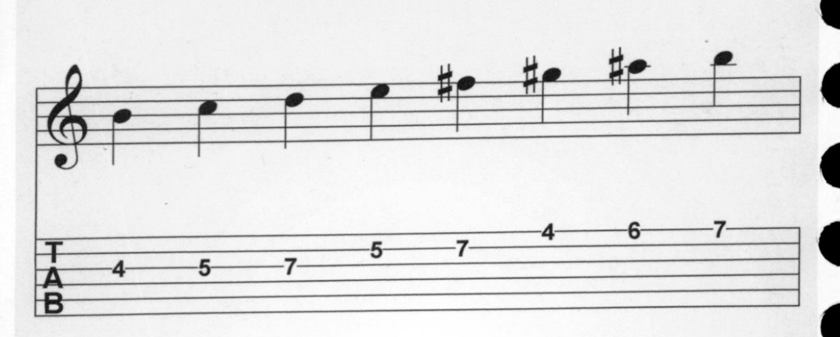


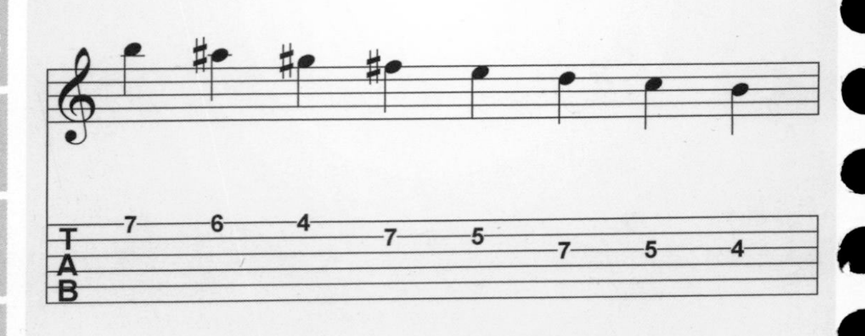


**Scale pattern**

B C D E F# G# A# B
B A# G# F# E D C B

# B Leading Wholetone

B
C
C♯/D♭
D
E♭/D♯
E
F
F♯/G♭
G
A♭/G♯

**Scale pattern**

B C♯ D♯ F G A A♯ B
B A♯ A♮ G F D♯ C♯ B

# B Lydian Augmented Dominant

| **Scale pattern** | B C♯ D♯ E♯ F× G♯ A B<br>B A G♯ F× E♯ D♯ C♯ B |
|---|---|

# B Lydian Dominant ♭6

| Scale pattern | B C♯ D♯ E♯ F♯ G A B |
| --- | --- |
| | B A G F♯ E♯ D♯ C♯ B |

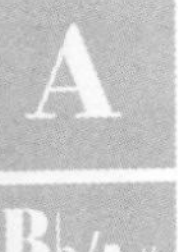



# B Major Locrian/Arabian

**Scale pattern**

B C♯ D♯ E F G A B

B A G F E D♯ C♯ B

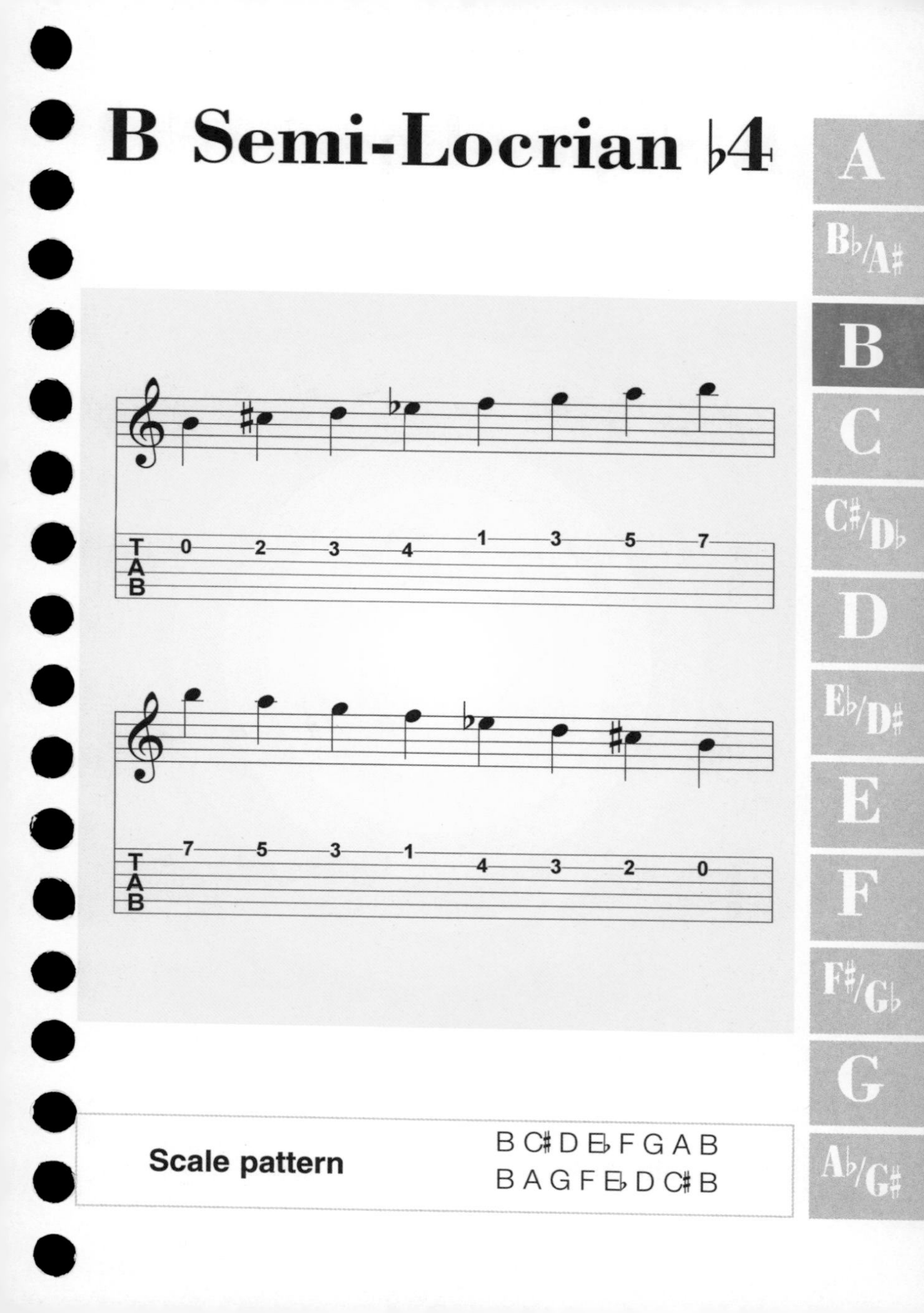
B Semi-Locrian ♭4
0 2 3 4 1 3 5 7
7 5 3 1 4 3 2 0
T
A
B
Scale pattern
B C♯ D E♭ F G A B
B A G F E♭ D C♯ B
A
B♭/A♯
B
C
C♯/D♭
D
E♭/D♯
E
F
F♯/G♭
G
A♭/G♯

# B Super-Locrian 𝄫3

**Scale pattern**

B C D♭ E♭ F G A B

B A G F E♭ D♭ C B

# B Bebop Dominant

**Scale pattern**

B C# D# E F# G# A A# B
B A# A♮ G# F# E D# C# B

A
B♭/A♯
B
C
C♯/D♭
D
E♭/D♯
E
F
F♯/G♭
G
A♭/G♯

# B Bebop Major

T
A
B
9 6 8 9 7 8 9 6 7

**Scale pattern**

B C♯ D♯ E F♯ G♮ G♯ A♯ B
B A♯ G♯ G♮ F♯ E D♯ C♯ B

# B Bebop Dorian

| Scale pattern | B C♯ D D♯ E F♯ G♯ A B<br>B A G♯ F♯ E D♯ D♮ C♯ B |
|---|---|

# B Byzantine/Arabic/ Double Harmonic Major

| **Scale pattern** | B C D♯ E F♯ G A♯ B<br>B A♯ G F♯ E D♯ C B |
|---|---|

# C Major

| | |
|---|---|
| **Scale pattern** | C D E F G A B C<br>C B A G F E D C |

A
B♭/A♯
B
C
C♯/D♭
D
E♭/D♯
E
F
F♯/G♭
G
A♭/G♯

# C Major Pentatonic

**Scale pattern**

C D E F G A B C
C B A G F E D C

# C Lydian

**Scale pattern**

C D E F♯ G A B C
C B A G F♯ E D C

# C Lydian Augmented

**Scale pattern**

C D E F♯ G♯ A B C
C B A G♯ F♯ E D C

# C Natural Minor

**Scale pattern**

C D E♭ F G A♭ B♭ C
C B♭ A♭ G F E♭ D C

A
B♭/A♯
B
C
C♯/D♭
D
E♭/D♯
E
F
F♯/G♭
G
A♭/G♯

A
B♭/A♯
B
C
C♯/D♭
D
E♭/D♯
E
F
F♯/G♭
G
A♭/G♯

# C Harmonic Minor

**Scale pattern**

C D E♭ F G A♭ B C
C B A♭ G F E♭ D C

# C Melodic Minor

| **Scale pattern** | C D E♭ F G A B C<br>C B♭ A♭ G F E♭ D C |
|---|---|

# C Dorian

| Scale pattern | C D E♭ F G A B♭ C<br>C B♭ A G F E♭ D C |
|---|---|

# C Minor Pentatonic

**Scale pattern**

C E♭ F G B♭ C
C B♭ G F E♭ C

A
B♭/A♯
B
C
C♯/D♭
D
E♭/D♯
E
F
F♯/G♭
G
A♭/G♯

# C Blues

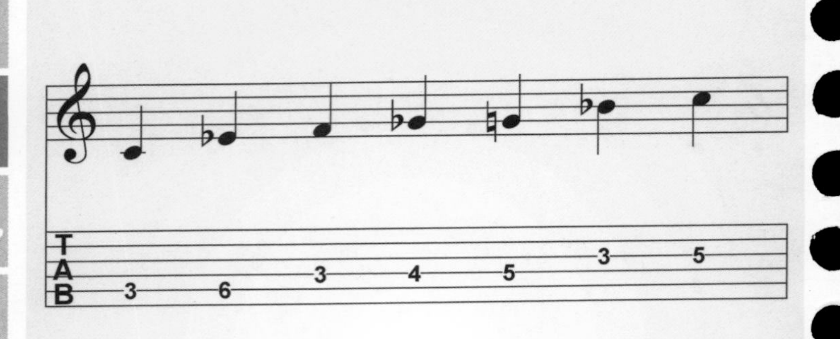

| **Scale pattern** | C E♭ F G♭ G♮ B♭ C<br>C B♭ G♮ G♭ F E♭ C |
|---|---|

# C Phrygian

**Scale pattern**

C D♭ E♭ F G A♭ B♭ C
C B♭ A♭ G F E♭ D♭ C

A
B♭/A♯
B
C
C♯/D♭
D
E♭/D♯
E
F
F♯/G♭
G
A♭/G♯

# C Locrian

**Scale pattern**

C D♭ E♭ F G♭ A♭ B♭ C

C B♭ A♭ G♭ F E♭ D♭ C

# C Half Diminished

**Scale pattern**

C D E♭ F G♭ A♭ B♭ C
C B♭ A♭ G♭ F E♭ D C

# C Mixolydian

**Scale pattern**

C D E F G A B♭ C
C B♭ A G F E D C

# C Phrygian Major/ Spanish Gypsy

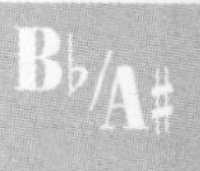


B
C
C♯/D♭
D
E♭/D♯
E
F
F♯/G♭
G
A♭/G♯

**Scale pattern**

C D♭ E F G A♭ B♭ C
C B♭ A♭ G F E D♭ C

# C Lydian Dominant

**Scale pattern**

C D E F♯ G A B♭ C
C B♭ A G F♯ E D C

# C Diminished Wholetone/ Super Locrian/Altered

T
A
B 3 4 1 2 4 1 3 1

T
A
B 1 3 1 4 2 1 4 3

**Scale pattern**

C D♭ E♭ F♭ G♭ A♭ B♭ C
C B♭ A♭ G♭ F♭ E♭ D♭ C

# C Diminished

**Scale pattern**

C D♭ E♭ E♮ F♯ G A B♭ C
C B♭ A G F♯ E♮ E♭ D♭ C

# C Chromatic

**Scale pattern**

C D♭ D♮ E♭ E♮ F F♯ G A♭ A♮ B♭ B♮ C

C B♮ B♭ A♮ A♭ G F♯ F♮ E♮ E♭ D♮ D♭ C

A
B♭/A♯
B
C
C♯/D♭
D
E♭/D♯
E
F
F♯/G♭
G
A♭/G♯

# C Wholetone

**Scale pattern**

C D E F♯ G♯ A♯ C
C A♯ G♯ F♯ E D C

A
B♭/A♯
B
C
C♯/D♭
D
E♭/D♯
E
F
F♯/G♭
G
A♭/G♯

# C Neapolitan

| **Scale pattern** | C D♭ E♭ F G A B C<br>C B A G F E♭ D♭ C |
|---|---|

# C Leading Wholetone

| **Scale pattern** | C D E F♯ G♯ A♯ B C<br>C B A♯ G♯ F♯ E D C |
|---|---|

# C Lydian Augmented Dominant

**Scale pattern**

C D E F♯ G♯ A B♭ C
C B♭ A G♯ F♯ E D C

A
B♭/A♯
B
C
C♯/D♭
D
E♭/D♯
E
F
F♯/G♭
G
A♭/G♯

# C Lydian Dominant ♭6

**Scale pattern**

C D E F♯ G A♭ B♭ C
C B♭ A♭ G F♯ E D C

# C Major Locrian/Arabian

**Scale pattern**

C D E F G♭ A♭ B♭ C

C B♭ A♭ G♭ F E D C

B♭/A#
B
C
C#/D♭
D
E♭/D#
E
F
F#/G♭
G
A♭/G#

# C Semi-Locrian ♭4

| Scale pattern | C D E♭ E♮ F# G# B♭ C<br>C B♭ G# F# E E♭ D C |
|---|---|

# C Super-Locrian 𝄫3

**Scale pattern**

C C♯ D E F♯ G♯ B♭ C
C B♭ G♯ F♯ E D D♭ C

A
B♭/A♯
B
C
C♯/D♭
D
E♭/D♯
E
F
F♯/G♭
G
A♭/G♯

# C Bebop Dominant

**Scale pattern**

C D E F G A B♭ B♮ C
C B B♭ A G F E D C

# C Bebop Major



T
A
B
3 5 2 3 5 1 2 4 1

T
A
B
1 4 2 1 5 3 2 5 3

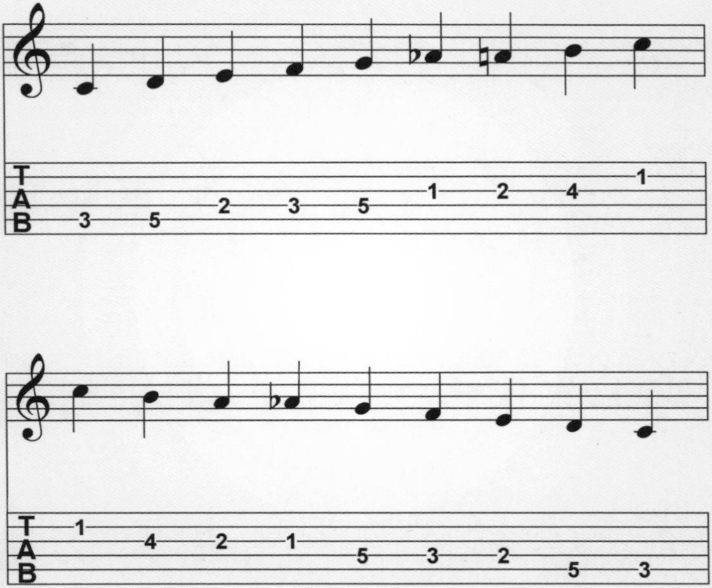

**Scale pattern**

C D E F G A♭ A♮ B C
C B A A♭ G F E D C

A
B♭/A♯
B
C
C♯/D♭
D
E♭/D♯
E
F
F♯/G♭
G
A♭/G♯

# C Bebop Dorian

**Scale pattern**

C D E♭ E♮ F G A B♭ C
C B♭ A G F E E♭ D C

# C Byzantine/Arabic/ Double Harmonic Major

T
A
B
3 4 2 3 5 6 4 5

T
A
B
5 4 6 5 3 2 4 3

**Scale pattern**

C D♭ E F G A♭ B C
C B A♭ G F E D♭ C

# D♭ Major

**Scale pattern**

D♭ E♭ F G♭ A♭ B♭ C D♭
D♭ C B♭ A♭ G♭ F E♭ D♭

# D♭ Major Pentatonic

**Scale pattern**

D♭ E♭ F A♭ B♭ D♭

D♭ B♭ A♭ F E♭ D♭

# D♭ Lydian

| **Scale pattern** | D♭ E♭ F G A♭ B♭ C D♭<br>D♭ C B♭ A♭ G F E♭ D♭ |
|---|---|

# D♭ Lydian Augmented

| **Scale pattern** | D♭ E♭ F G A B♭ C D♭<br>D♭ C B♭ A G F E♭ D♭ |
|---|---|

# C♯ Natural Minor

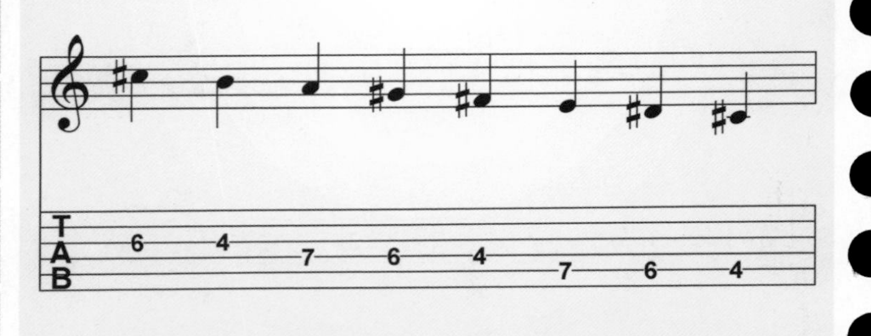


**Scale pattern**

C♯ D♯ E F♯ G♯ A B C♯
C♯ B A G♯ F♯ E D♯ C♯

# C♯ Harmonic Minor

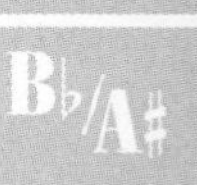

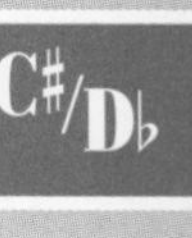

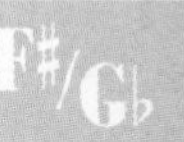

**Scale pattern**

C♯ D♯ E F♯ G♯ A B♯ C♯
C♯ B♯ A G♯ F♯ E D♯ C♯

# C♯ Melodic Minor

| **Scale pattern** | C♯ D♯ E F♯ G♯ A♯ B♯ C♯<br>C♯ B♮ A♮ G♯ F♯ E D♯ C♯ |
|---|---|

# C♯ Dorian

| **Scale pattern** | C♯ D♯ E F♯ G♯ A♯ B C♯<br>C♯ B A♯ G♯ F♯ E D♯ C♯ |
|---|---|

# C♯ Minor Pentatonic

**Scale pattern**

C♯ E F♯ G♯ B C♯
C♯ B G♯ F♯ E C♯

# C♯ Blues

| **Scale pattern** | C♯ E F♯ G♮ G♯ B C♯ |
| --- | --- |
| | C♯ B G♯ G♮ F♯ E C♯ |

# C♯ Phrygian

| **Scale pattern** | C♯ D E F♯ G♯ A B C♯<br>C♯ B A G♯ F♯ E D C♯ |
|---|---|

# C♯ Locrian

**Scale pattern**

C♯ D E F♯ G A B C♯
C♯ B A G F♯ E D C♯

# C♯ Half Diminished

**Scale pattern**

C♯ D♯ E F♯ G A B C♯
C♯ B A G F♯ E D♯ C♯

# C♯ Mixolydian

**Scale pattern**

C♯ D♯ E♯ F♯ G♯ A♯ B C♯
C♯ B A♯ G♯ F♯ E♯ D♯ C♯

# C♯ Phrygian Major/ Spanish Gypsy

| **Scale pattern** | C♯ D E♯ F♯ G♯ A B C♯<br>C♯ B A G♯ F♯ E♯ D C♯ |
|---|---|

# D♭ Lydian Dominant

**Scale pattern**

D♭ E♭ F G A♭ B♭ C♭ D♭

D♭ C♭ B♭ A♭ G F E♭ D♭

# C♯ Diminished Wholetone/ Super Locrian/Altered

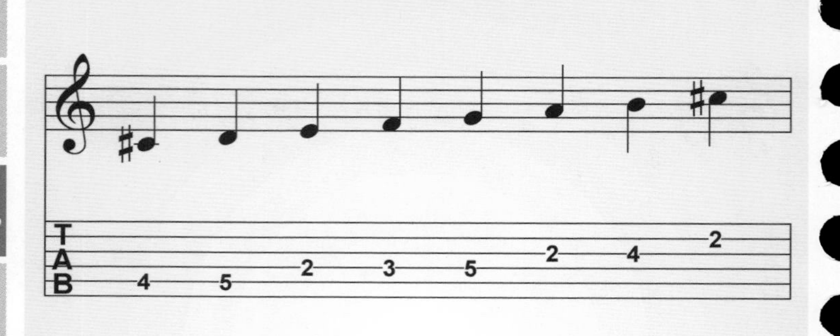

**Scale pattern**

C♯ D E F G A B C♯
C♯ B A G F E D C♯

# C♯ Diminished

**Scale pattern**

C♯ D E F G G♯ A♯ B C♯
C♯ B A♯ G♯ G♮ F E D C♯

A
B♭/A♯
B
C
C♯/D♭
D
E♭/D♯
E
F
F♯/G♭
G
A♭/G♯

# C♯ Chromatic

**Scale pattern**

C♯ D D♯ E E♯ F♯ F× G♯ A A♯ B B♯ C♯

C♯ B♯ B♮ A♯ A♮ G♯ F× F♯ E♯ E♮ D♯ D♮ C♯

# D♭ Wholetone

T
A
B
4 6 3 5 2 4 2

T
A
B
2 4 2 5 3 6 4

**Scale pattern**

D♭ E♭ F G A B D♭
D♭ B A G F E♭ D♭

A
B♭/A♯
B
C
C♯/D♭
D
E♭/D♯
E
F
F♯/G♭
G
A♭/G♯

# C♯ Neapolitan

T
A
B
4 5 2 4 6 3 5 6

**Scale pattern**

C♯ D E F♯ G♯ A♯ B♯ C♯
C♯ B♯ A♯ G♯ F♯ E D C♯

# D♭ Leading Wholetone

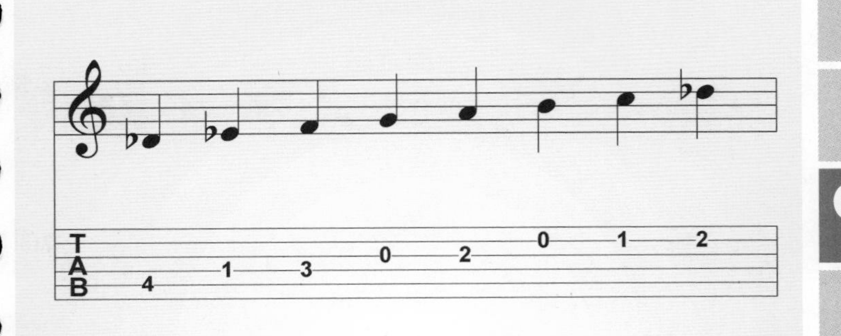

**Scale pattern**

D♭ E♭ F G A B C D♭
D♭ C B A G F E♭ D♭

B♭/A♯
B
C
C♯/D♭
D
E♭/D♯
E
F
F♯/G♭
G
A♭/G♯

# D♭ Lydian Augmented Dominant

**Scale pattern**

D♭ E♭ F G A B♭ C♭ D♭
D♭ C♭ B♭ A G F E♭ D♭

# D♭ Lydian Dominant ♭6

**Scale pattern**

D♭ E♭ F G A♭ B♭♭ C♭ D♭

D♭ C♭ B♭♭ A♭ G F E♭ D♭

# C♯ Major Locrian/Arabian

**Scale pattern**

C♯ D♯ E♯ F♯ G A B C♯
C♯ B A G F♯ E♯ D♯ C♯

# C♯ Semi-Locrian ♭4

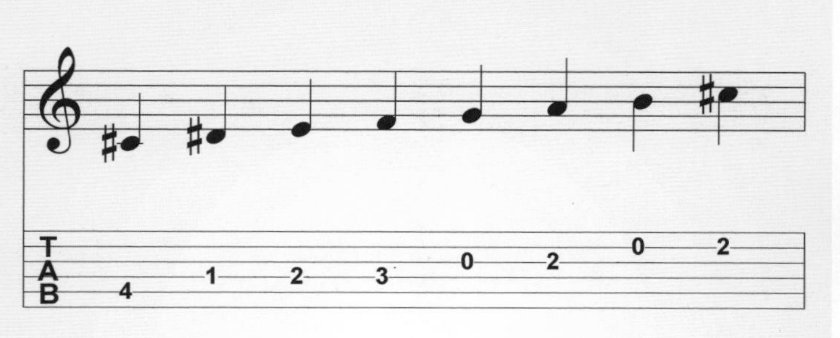

**Scale pattern**

C♯ D♯ E F G A B C♯
C♯ B A G F E D♯ C♯

A
B♭/A♯
B
C
C♯/D♭
D
E♭/D♯
E
F
F♯/G♭
G
A♭/G♯

# C♯ Super-Locrian 𝄫3

**Scale pattern**

C♯ D E𝄫 F G A B C♯
C♯ B A G F E𝄫 D C♯

# D♭ Bebop Dominant

**Scale pattern**

D♭ E♭ F G♭ A♭ B♭ C♭ C♮ D♭
D♭ C C♭ B♭ A♭ G♭ F E♭ D♭

B
C
C♯/D♭
D
E♭/D♯
E
F
F♯/G♭
G
A♭/G♯

# C♯ Bebop Major

**Scale pattern**

C♯ D♯ E♯ F♯ G♯ A♮ A♯ B♯ C♯
C♯ B♯ A♯ A♮ G♯ F♯ E♯ D♯ C♯

# C♯ Bebop Dorian

A
B♭/A♯
B
C
C♯/D♭
D
E♭/D♯
E
F
F♯/G♭
G
A♭/G♯

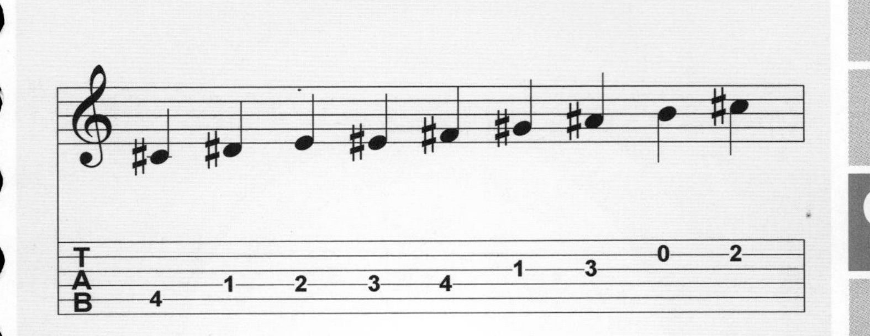

**Scale pattern**

C♯ D♯ E E♯ F♯ G♯ A♯ B C♯

C♯ B A♯ G♯ F♯ E♯ E♮ D♯ C♯

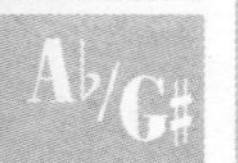


# C♯ Byzantine/Arabic/ Double Harmonic Major

| Scale pattern | C♯ D E♯ F♯ G♯ A B♯ C♯<br>C♯ B♯ A G♯ F♯ E♯ D C♯ |
|---|---|

# D Major

| **Scale pattern** | D E F♯ G A B C♯ D<br>D C♯ B A G F♯ E D |
|---|---|

# D Major Pentatonic

**Scale pattern**

D E F♯ A B D
D B A F♯ E D

# D Lydian

**Scale pattern**

D E F♯ G♯ A B C♯ D
D C♯ B A G♯ F♯ E D

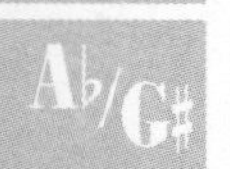


# D Lydian Augmented

**Scale pattern**

D E F♯ G♯ A♯ B C♯ D
D C♯ B A♯ G♯ F♯ E D

# D Natural Minor

**Scale pattern**

D E F G A B♭ C D
D C B♭ A G F E D

# D Harmonic Minor

T
A
B
5 7 8 5 7 8 6 7

**Scale pattern**

D E F G A B♭ C♯ D
D C♯ B♭ A G F E D

# D Melodic Minor

**Scale pattern**

D E F G A B C♯ D
D C♮ B♭ A G F E D

# D Dorian

**Scale pattern**

D E F G A B C D
D C B A G F E D

# D Minor Pentatonic

| Scale pattern | D F G A C D<br>D C A G F D |
| --- | --- |

# D Blues

| **Scale pattern** | D F G A♭ A♮ C D<br>D C A♮ A♭ G F D |
| --- | --- |

# D Phrygian

**Scale pattern**

D E♭ F G A B♭ C D
D C B♭ A G F E♭ D

# D Locrian

| **Scale pattern** | D E♭ F G A♭ B♭ C D<br>D C B♭ A♭ G F E♭ D |
|---|---|

# D Half Diminished

**Scale pattern**

D E F G A♭ B♭ C D
D C B♭ A♭ G F E D

# D Mixolydian

**Scale pattern**

D E F♯ G A B C D
D C B A G F♯ E D

# D Phrygian Major/ Spanish Gypsy

T
A
B
0 1 4 0 2 3 1 3

T
A
B
3 1 3 2 0 4 1 0

**Scale pattern**

D E♭ F♯ G A B♭ C D
D C B♭ A G F♯ E♭ D

# D Lydian Dominant

**Scale pattern**

D E F♯ G♯ A B C D
D C B A G♯ F♯ E D

# D Diminished Wholetone/ Super Locrian/Altered

| | |
|---|---|
| Scale pattern | D E♭ F G♭ A♭ B♭ C D<br>D C B♭ A♭ G♭ F E♭ D |

# D Diminished

TAB 5 6 3 4 6 7 4 5 7

| **Scale pattern** | D E♭ F F♯ G♯ A B C D<br>D C B A G♯ F♯ F♮ E♭ D |
|---|---|

# D Chromatic

**Scale pattern**

D E♭ E♮ F F♯ G G♯ A B♭ B♮ C C♯ D

D C♯ C♮ B B♭ A G♯ G♮ F♯ F♮ E E♭ D

# D Wholetone

| **Scale pattern** | D E F♯ G♯ A♯ C D<br>D C A♯ G♯ F♯ E D |
|---|---|

# D Neapolitan

| T | | | | | | | | |
|---|---|---|---|---|---|---|---|---|
| A | | | | | | 4 | 6 | 7 |
| | | | 3 | 5 | 7 | | | |
| B | 5 | 6 | | | | | | |

| T | | | | | | | | |
|---|---|---|---|---|---|---|---|---|
| A | 7 | 6 | 4 | | | | | |
| | | | | 7 | 5 | 3 | | |
| B | | | | | | | 6 | 5 |

**Scale pattern**

D E♭ F G A B C♯ D
D C♯ B A G F E♭ D

# D Leading Wholetone

**Scale pattern**

D E F♯ G♯ A♯ B♯ C♯ D
D C♯ B♯ A♯ G♯ F♯ E D

# D Lydian Augmented Dominant

**Scale pattern**

D E F♯ G♯ A♯ B C D
D C B A♯ G♯ F♯ E D

A
B♭/A♯
B
C
C♯/D♭
D
E♭/D♯
E
F
F♯/G♭
G
A♭/G♯

# D Lydian Dominant ♭6

**Scale pattern**

D E F♯ G♯ A B♭ C D
D C B♭ A G♯ F♯ E D

# D Major
# Locrian/Arabian

| Scale pattern | D E F♯ G A♭ B♭ C D<br>D C B♭ A♭ G F♯ E D |
|---|---|

B
C
C♯/D♭
D
E♭/D♯
E
F
F♯/G♭
G
A♭/G♯

# D Semi-Locrian ♭4

**Scale pattern**

D E F G♭ A♭ B♭ C D
D C B♭ A♭ G♭ F E D

# D Super-Locrian ♭♭3

| **Scale pattern** | D D♯ E F♯ G♯ B♭ C D<br>D C B♭ G♯ F♯ E E♭ D |
|---|---|

A
B♭/A♯
B
C
C♯/D♭
D
E♭/D♯
E
F
F♯/G♭
G
A♭/G♯

# D Bebop Dominant

| **Scale pattern** | D E F♯ G A B C C♯ D<br>D C♯ C♮ B A G F♯ E D |
|---|---|

# D Bebop Major

**Scale pattern**

D E F♯ G A B♭ B♮ C♯ D
D C♯ B B♭ A G F♯ E D

A
B♭/A♯
B
C
C♯/D♭
D
E♭/D♯
E
F
F♯/G♭
G
A♭/G♯

# D Bebop Dorian

**Scale pattern**

D E F F♯ G A B C D
D C B A G F♯ F♮ E D

# D Byzantine/Arabic/ Double Harmonic Major

| Scale pattern | D E♭ F♯ G A B♭ C♯ D<br>D C♯ B♭ A G F♯ E♭ D |
|---|---|

# E♭ Major

**Scale pattern**

E♭ F G A♭ B♭ C D E♭

E♭ D C B♭ A♭ G F E♭

# E♭ Major Pentatonic

**Scale pattern**

E♭ F G B♭ C E♭

E♭ C B♭ G F E♭

# E♭ Lydian

| Scale pattern | E♭ F G A B♭ C D E♭<br>E♭ D C B♭ A G F E♭ |
|---|---|

# E♭ Lydian Augmented

| Scale pattern | E♭ F G A B C D E♭ |
| --- | --- |
| | E♭ D C B A G F E♭ |

B
C
C♯/D♭
D
E♭/D♯
E
F
F♯/G♭
G
A♭/G♯

# E♭ Natural Minor

**Scale pattern**

E♭ F G♭ A♭ B♭ C♭ D♭ E♭
E♭ D♭ C♭ B♭ A♭ G♭ F E♭

# E♭ Harmonic Minor

| **Scale pattern** | E♭ F G♭ A♭ B♭ C♭ D E♭<br>E♭ D C♭ B♭ A♭ G♭ F E♭ |
|---|---|

# E♭ Melodic Minor

**Scale pattern**

E♭ F G♭ A♭ B♭ C D E♭

E♭ D♭ C♭ B♭ A♭ G♭ F E♭

# E♭ Dorian

| Scale pattern | E♭ F G♭ A♭ B♭ C D♭ E♭ |
|---|---|
| | E♭ D♭ C B♭ A♭ G♭ F E♭ |

# E♭ Minor Pentatonic

**Scale pattern**

E♭ G♭ A♭ B♭ D♭ E♭
E♭ D♭ B♭ A♭ G♭ E♭

# D♯ Blues

T
A
B
1 4 1 2 3 2 4

T
A
B
4 2 3 2 1 4 1

| Scale pattern | D♯ F♯ G♯ A♮ A♯ C♯ D♯ |
| --- | --- |
| | D♯ C♯ A♯ A♮ G♯ F♯ D♯ |

A
B♭/A♯
B
C
C♯/D♭
D
E♭/D♯
E
F
F♯/G♭
G
A♭/G♯

# D♯ Phrygian

**Scale pattern**

D♯ E F♯ G♯ A♯ B C♯ D♯
D♯ C♯ B A♯ G♯ F♯ E D♯

# D♯ Locrian

**Scale pattern**

D♯ E F♯ G♯ A B C♯ D♯
D♯ C♯ B A G♯ F♯ E D♯

# D♯ Half Diminished

**Scale pattern**

D♯ E♯ F♯ G♯ A B C♯ D♯

D♯ C♯ B A G♯ F♯ E♯ D♯

# E♭ Mixolydian

**Scale pattern**

E♭ F G A♭ B♭ C D♭ E♭
E♭ D♭ C B♭ A♭ G F E♭

A
B♭/A♯
B
C
C♯/D♭
D
E♭/D♯
E
F
F♯/G♭
G
A♭/G♯

# E♭ Phrygian Major/ Spanish Gypsy

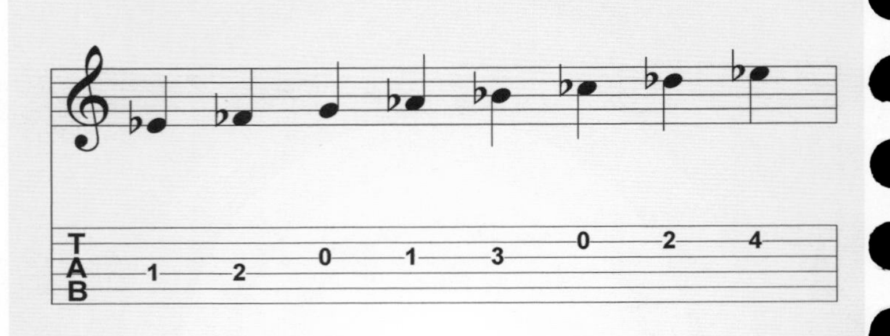

**Scale pattern**

E♭ F♭ G A♭ B♭ C♭ D♭ E♭

E♭ D♭ C♭ B♭ A♭ G F♭ E♭

# E♭ Lydian Dominant

**Scale pattern**

E♭ F G A B♭ C D♭ E♭
E♭ D♭ C B♭ A G F E♭

A
B♭/A♯
B
C
C♯/D♭
D
E♭/D♯
E
F
F♯/G♭
G
A♭/G♯

# D♯ Diminished Wholetone/ Super Locrian/Altered

**Scale pattern**

D♯ E F♯ G A B C♯ D♯
D♯ C♯ B A G F♯ E D♯

# E♭ Diminished

T A B 1 2 4 5 2 3 5 2 4

**Scale pattern**

E♭ F♭ G♭ G♮ A B♭ C D♭ E♭

E♭ D♭ C B♭ A G G♭ F♭ E♭

A
B♭/A♯
B
C
C♯/D♭
D
E♭/D♯
E
F
F♯/G♭
G
A♭/G♯

# E♭ Chromatic

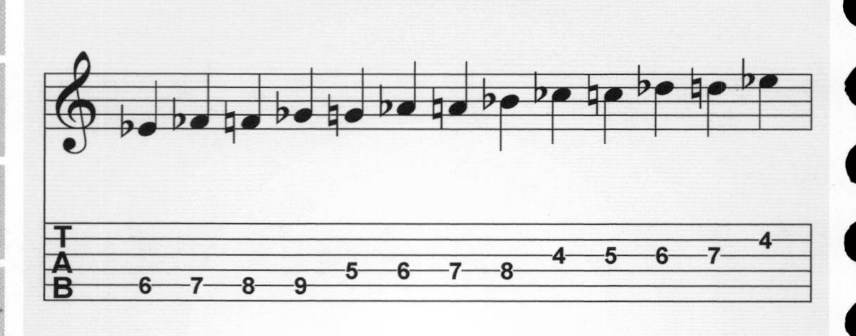

**Scale pattern**

E♭ F♭ F♮ G♭ G♮ A♭ A♮ B♭ C♭ C♮ D♭ D♮ E♭

E♭ D D♭ C C♭ B♭ A A♭ G G♭ F F♭ E♭

# E♭ Wholetone

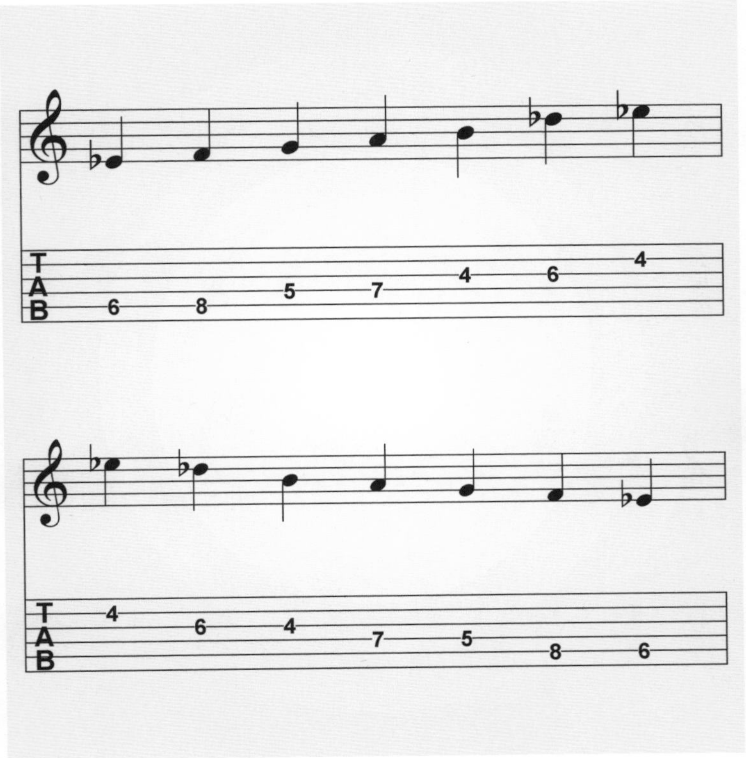

T
A
B 6 8 5 7 4 6 4

T
A
B 4 6 4 7 5 8 6

**Scale pattern**

E♭ F G A B D♭ E♭
E♭ D♭ B A G F E♭

A
B♭/A#
B
C
C#/D♭
D
E♭/D#
E
F
F#/G♭
G
A♭/G#

# E♭ Neapolitan

**Scale pattern**

E♭ F♭ G♭ A♭ B♭ C D E♭
E♭ D C B♭ A♭ G♭ F♭ E♭

# E♭ Leading Wholetone

| | |
|---|---|
| **Scale pattern** | E♭ F G A B C♯ D E♭<br>E♭ D C♯ B A G F E♭ |

A
B♭/A♯
B
C
C♯/D♭
D
E♭/D♯
E
F
F♯/G♭
G
A♭/G♯

# E♭ Lydian Augmented Dominant

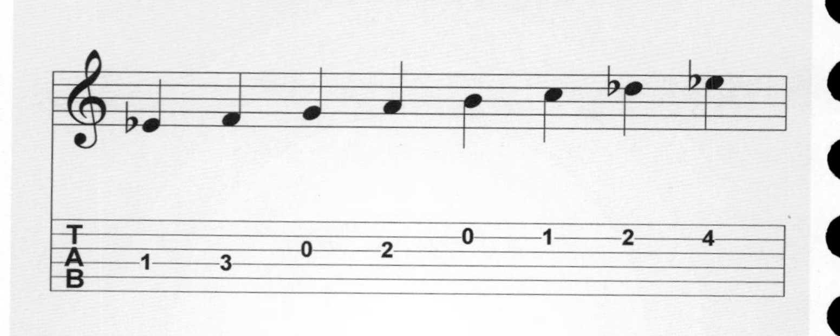

**Scale pattern**

E♭ F G A B C D♭ E♭
E♭ D♭ C B A G F E♭

# E♭ Lydian Dominant ♭6

| Scale pattern | E♭ F G A B♭ C♭ D♭ E♭<br>E♭ D♭ C♭ B♭ A G F E♭ |
| --- | --- |

# D♯ Major Locrian/Arabian

**Scale pattern**

D♯ E♯ F× G♯ A B C♯ D♯

D♯ C♯ B A G♯ F× E♯ D♯

# E♭ Semi-Locrian ♭4

**Scale pattern**

E♭ F F♯ G A B D♭ E♭
E♭ D♭ B A G G♭ F E♭

# D♯ Super-Locrian 𝄫3

T
A
B
1 2 3 0 2 0 2 4

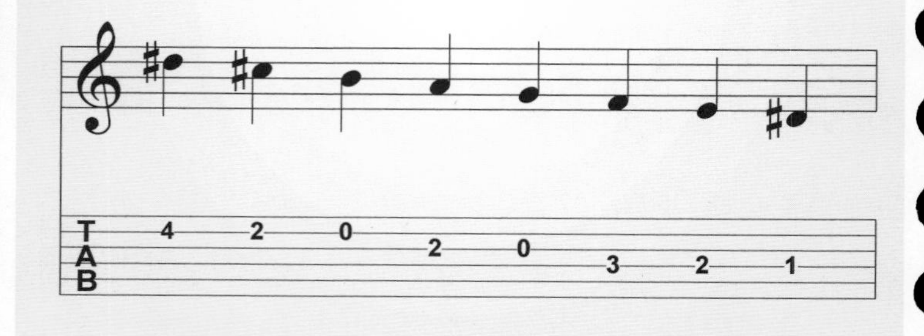


| **Scale pattern** | D♯ E F G A B C♯ D♯<br>D♯ C♯ B A G F E D♯ |
|---|---|

A
B♭/A♯
B
C
C♯/D♭
D
E♭/D♯
E
F
F♯/G♭
G
A♭/G♯

# E♭ Bebop Dominant

| Scale pattern | E♭ F G A♭ B♭ C D♭ D♮ E♭<br>E♭ D D♭ C B♭ A♭ G F E♭ |
|---|---|

# E♭ Bebop Major

**Scale pattern**

E♭ F G A♭ B♭ C♭ C♮ D E♭
E♭ D C C♭ B♭ A♭ G F E♭

# E♭ Bebop Dorian

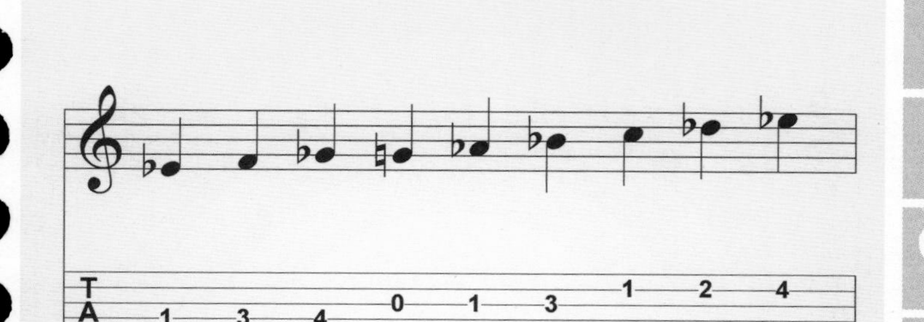

**Scale pattern**

E♭ F G♭ G♮ A♭ B♭ C D♭ E♭

E♭ D♭ C B♭ A♭ G G♭ F E♭

# E♭ Byzantine/Arabic/ Double Harmonic Major

**Scale pattern**

E♭ F♭ G A♭ B♭ C♭ D E♭
E♭ D C♭ B♭ A♭ G F♭ E♭

# E Major

| Scale pattern | E F♯ G♯ A B C♯ D♯ E<br>E D♯ C♯ B A G♯ F♯ E |
|---|---|

# E Major Pentatonic

| **Scale pattern** | E F♯ G♯ B C♯ E<br>E C♯ B G♯ F♯ E |
|---|---|

# E Lydian

| **Scale pattern** | E F♯ G♯ A♯ B C♯ D♯ E<br>E D♯ C♯ B A♯ G♯ F♯ E |
|---|---|

# E Lydian Augmented

| **Scale pattern** | E F# G# A# B# C# D# E<br>E D# C# B# A# G# F# E |
|---|---|

# E Natural Minor

**Scale pattern**

E F# G A B C D E
E D C B A G F# E

# E Harmonic Minor

T
A
B
2 4 5 2 4 5 4 5

| **Scale pattern** | E F♯ G A B C D♯ E<br>E D♯ C B A G F♯ E |
|---|---|

# E Melodic Minor

T
A
B

2 4 5 2 4 2 4 5

T
A
B

5 3 5 4 2 5 4 2

**Scale pattern**

E F♯ G A B C♯ D♯ E
E D♮ C♮ B A G F♯ E

# E Dorian

**Scale pattern**

E F♯ G A B C D♯ E
E D C♯ B A G F♯ E

# E Minor Pentatonic

**Scale pattern**

E G A B D E
E D B A G E

# E Blues

TAB
2 5 2 3 4 3 5

| **Scale pattern** | E G A B♭ B♮ D E<br>E D B♮ B♭ A G E |
|---|---|

# E Phrygian



**Scale pattern**

E F G A B C D E
E D C B A G F E

A
B♭/A♯
B
C
C♯/D♭
D
E♭/D♯
E
F
F♯/G♭
G
A♭/G♯

# E Locrian

**Scale pattern**

E F G A B♭ C D E
E D C B♭ A G F E

# E Half Diminished

**Scale pattern**

E F♯ G A B♭ C D E
E D C B♭ A G F♯ E

# E Mixolydian

**Scale pattern**

E F♯ G♯ A B C♯ D E
E D C♯ B A G♯ F♯ E

# E Phrygian Major/ Spanish Gypsy

**Scale pattern**

E F G♯ A B C D E
E D C B A G♯ F E

# E Lydian Dominant

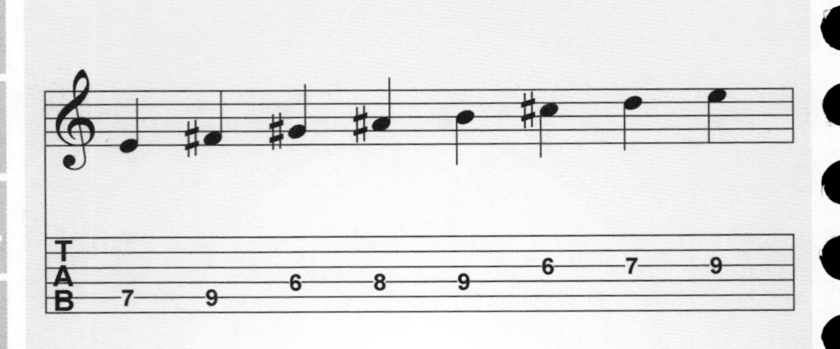

**Scale pattern**

E F♯ G♯ A♯ B C♯ D E
E D C♯ B A♯ G♯ F♯ E

E Diminished Wholetone/
Super Locrian/Altered
T
A
B
7 8 5 6 8 5 7 5
T
A
B
5 7 5 8 6 5 8 7
Scale pattern
E F G A♭ B♭ C D E
E D C B♭ A♭ G F E
A
B♭/A#
B
C
C#/D♭
D
E♭/D#
E
F
F#/G♭
G
A♭/G#

# E Diminished

**Scale pattern**

E F G G♯ A♯ B C♯ D E
E D C♯ B A♯ G♯ G♮ F E

# E Chromatic

**Scale pattern**

E F F♯ G G♯ A A♯ B C C♯ D D♯ E

E D♯ D♮ C♯ C♮ B A♯ A♮ G♯ G♮ F♯ F♮ E

A
B♭/A♯
B
C
C♯/D♭
D
E♭/D♯
E
F
F♯/G♭
G
A♭/G♯

# E Wholetone

**Scale pattern**

E F♯ G♯ A♯ C D E
E D C A♯ G♯ F♯ E

# E Neapolitan

**Scale pattern**

E F G A B C♯ D♯ E
E D♯ C♯ B A G F E

# E Leading Wholetone

| **Scale pattern** | E F♯ G♯ B♭ C D D♯ E<br>E D♯ D♮ C B♭ G♯ F♯ E |
|---|---|

# E Lydian Augmented Dominant

**Scale pattern**

E F# G# A# B# C# D E
E D C# B# A# G# F# E

# E Lydian Dominant ♭6

**Scale pattern**

E F♯ G♯ A♯ B C D E
E D C B A♯ G♯ F♯ E

# E Major Locrian/Arabian

| **Scale pattern** | E F♯ G♯ A B♭ C D E<br>E D C B♭ A G♯ F♯ E |
|---|---|

# E Semi-Locrian ♭4

T
A
B
2 4 0 1 3 1 3 0

**Scale pattern**

E F♯ G A♭ B♭ C D E
E D C B♭ A♭ G F♯ E

# E Super-Locrian 𝄫3

**Scale pattern**

E F G♭ A♭ B♭ C D E
E D C B♭ A♭ G♭ F E

A
B♭/A♯
B
C
C♯/D♭
D
E♭/D♯
E
F
F♯/G♭
G
A♭/G♯

# E Bebop Dominant

| Scale pattern | E F♯ G♯ A B C♯ D D♯ E<br>E D♯ D♮ C♯ B A G♯ F♯ E |
|---|---|

# E Bebop Major

**Scale pattern**

E F♯ G♯ A B C♮ C♯ D♯ E
E D♯ C♯ C♮ B A G♯ F♯ E

A
B♭/A♯
B
C
C♯/D♭
D
E♭/D♯
E
F
F♯/G♭
G
A♭/G♯

# E Bebop Dorian

| **Scale pattern** | E F♯ G G♯ A B C♯ D E<br>E D C♯ B A G♯ G♮ F♯ E |
|---|---|

# E Byzantine/Arabic/ Double Harmonic Major

| Scale pattern | E F G♯ A B C D♯ E<br>E D♯ C B A G♯ F E |
|---|---|

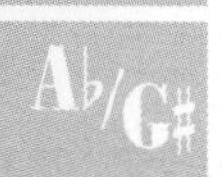

# F Major

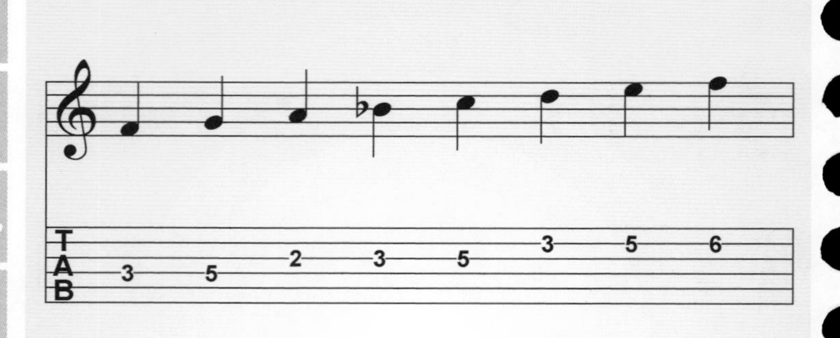

**Scale pattern**

F G A B♭ C D E F
F E D C B♭ A G F

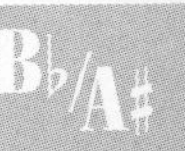


# F Major Pentatonic

| **Scale pattern** | F G A C D F<br>F D C A G F |
|---|---|

# F Lydian

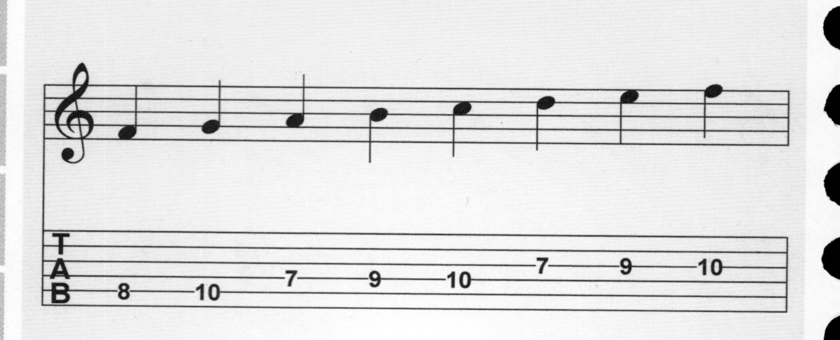

**Scale pattern**

F G A B C D E F
F E D C B A G F

# F Lydian Augmented

| Scale pattern | F G A B C♯ D E F<br>F E D C♯ B A G F |
|---|---|

A
B♭/A♯
B
C
C♯/D♭
D
E♭/D♯
E
F
F♯/G♭
G
A♭/G♯

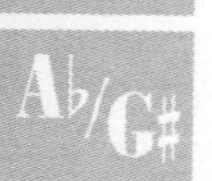

# F Natural Minor

**Scale pattern**

F G A♭ B♭ C D♭ E♭ F
F E♭ D♭ C B♭ A♭ G F

# F Harmonic Minor

T
A 3 5 6 3 5 6 5 6
B

T 6 5 6 5 3 6 5 3
A
B

**Scale pattern**

F G A♭ B♭ C D♭ E F
F E D♭ C B♭ A♭ G F

A
B♭/A♯
B
C
C♯/D♭
D
E♭/D♯
E
F
F♯/G♭
G
A♭/G♯

# F Melodic Minor

**Scale pattern**

F G A♭ B♭ C D E F
F E♭ D♭ C B♭ A♭ G F

# F Dorian

**Scale pattern**

F G A♭ B♭ C D E♭ F
F E♭ D C B♭ A♭ G F

# F Minor Pentatonic

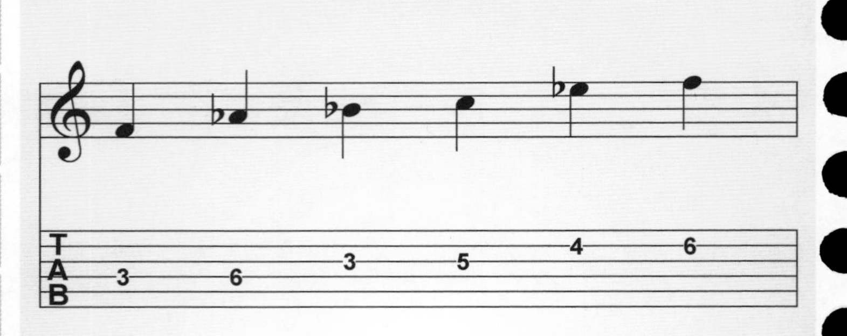

**Scale pattern**

F A♭ B♭ C E♭ F

F E♭ C B♭ A♭ F

# F Blues

| **Scale pattern** | F A♭ B♭ C♭ C♮ E♭ F<br>F E♭ C♮ C♭ B♭ A♭ F |
|---|---|

A
B♭/A#
B
C
C#/D♭
D
E♭/D#
E
F
F#/G♭
G
A♭/G#

# F Phrygian

**Scale pattern**

F G♭ A♭ B♭ C D♭ E♭ F
F E♭ D♭ C B♭ A♭ G♭ F

# F Locrian

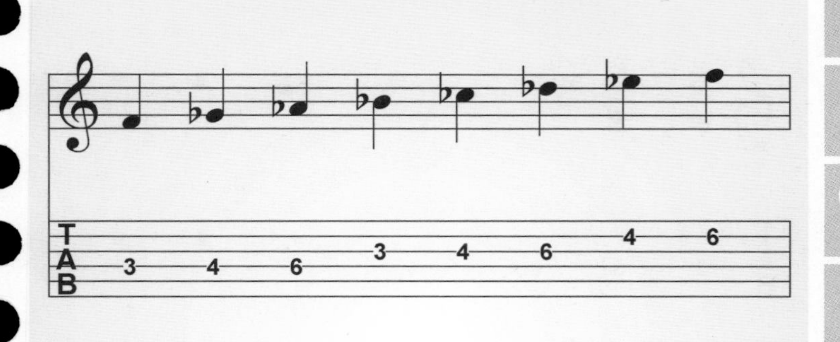

**Scale pattern**

F G♭ A♭ B♭ C♭ D♭ E♭ F
F E♭ D♭ C♭ B♭ A♭ G♭ F

A
B♭/A♯
B
C
C♯/D♭
D
E♭/D♯
E
F
F♯/G♭
G
A♭/G♯

# F Half Diminished

**Scale pattern**

F G A♭ B♭ C♭ D♭ E♭ F
F E♭ D♭ C♭ B♭ A♭ G F

# F Mixolydian

| **Scale pattern** | F G A B♭ C D E♭ F<br>F E♭ D C B♭ A G F |
|---|---|

# F Phrygian Major/ Spanish Gypsy

**Scale pattern**

F G♭ A B♭ C D♭ E♭ F
F E♭ D♭ C B♭ A G♭ F

# F Lydian Dominant

| Scale pattern | F G A B C D E♭ F<br>F E♭ D C B A G F |
|---|---|

# F Diminished Wholetone/ Super Locrian/Altered

**Scale pattern**

F G♭ A♭ B♭♭ C♭ D♭ E♭ F
F E♭ D♭ C♭ B♭♭ A♭ G♭ F

# F Diminished

**Scale pattern**

F G♭ A♭ A♮ B C D E♭ F
F E♭ D C B A A♭ G♭ F

# F Chromatic

**Scale pattern**

F G♭ G♮ A♭ A♮ B♭ B♮ C D♭ D♮ E♭ E♮ F

F E E♭ D D♭ C B B♭ A A♭ G G♭ F

# F Wholetone

**Scale pattern**

F G A B C♯ D♯ F
F D♯ C♯ B A G F

# F Neapolitan

**Scale pattern**

F G♭ A♭ B♭ C D E F
F E D C B♭ A♭ G♭ F

# F Leading Wholetone

**Scale pattern**

F G A B C♯ D♯ E F
F E D♯ C♯ B A G F

# F Lydian Augmented Dominant

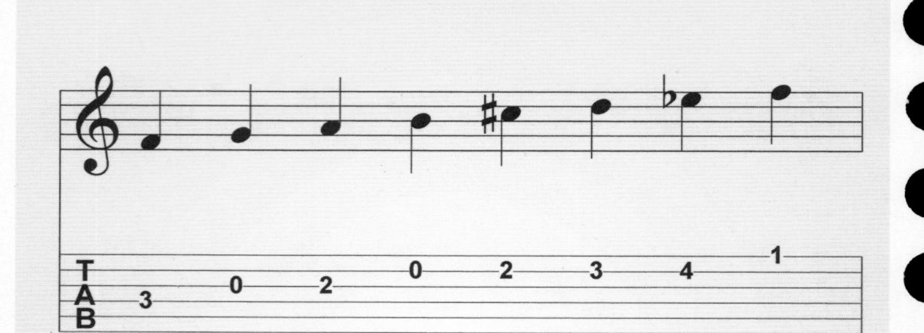

**Scale pattern**

F G A B C♯ D E♭ F
F E♭ D C♯ B A G F

# F Lydian Dominant ♭6

B
C
C#/D♭
D
E♭/D#
E
F
F#/G♭
G
A♭/G#

| Scale pattern | F G A B C D♭ E♭ F<br>F E♭ D♭ C B A G F |
|---|---|

# F Major Locrian/Arabian

**Scale pattern**

F G A B♭ C♭ D♭ E♭ F
F E♭ D♭ C♭ B♭ A G F

# F Semi-Locrian ♭4

T
A
B
3 0 1 2 0 2 4 1

T
A
B
1 4 2 0 2 1 0 3

**Scale pattern**

F G G♯ A B C♯ E♭ F
F E♭ C♯ B A A♭ G F

# F Super-Locrian ♭♭3

| **Scale pattern** | F F♯ G A B C♯ E♭ F<br>F E♭ C♯ B A G G♭ F |
| --- | --- |

# F Bebop Dominant

**Scale pattern**

F G A B♭ C D E♭ E♮ F
F E E♭ D C B♭ A G F

# F Bebop Major

**Scale pattern**

F G A B♭ C D♭ D♮ E F
F E D D♭ C B♭ A G F

# F Bebop Dorian

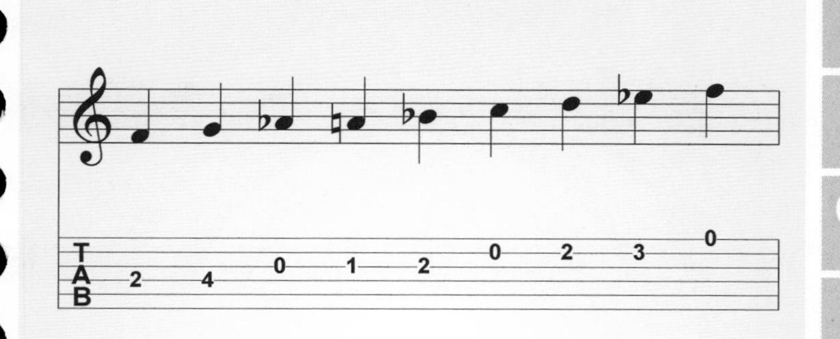

**Scale pattern**

F G A♭ A♮ B♭ C D E♭ F
F E♭ D C B♭ A A♭ G F

A
B♭/A♯
B
C
C♯/D♭
D
E♭/D♯
E
F
F♯/G♭
G
A♭/G♯

# F Byzantine/Arabic/ Double Harmonic Major

| **Scale pattern** | F G♭ A B♭ C D♭ E F<br>F E D♭ C B♭ A G♭ F |
|---|---|

# F♯ Major

**Scale pattern**

F♯ G♯ A♯ B C♯ D♯ E♯ F♯
F♯ E♯ D♯ C♯ B A♯ G♯ F♯

# F♯ Major Pentatonic

**Scale pattern**

F♯ G♯ A♯ C♯ D♯ F♯
F♯ D♯ C♯ A♯ G♯ F♯

# G♭ Lydian

**Scale pattern**

G♭ A♭ B♭ C D♭ E♭ F G♭

G♭ F E♭ D♭ C B♭ A♭ G♭

# G♭ Lydian Augmented

| Scale pattern | G♭ A♭ B♭ C D E♭ F G♭ |
|---|---|
| | G♭ F E♭ D C B♭ A♭ G♭ |

# F♯ Natural Minor

**Scale pattern**

F♯ G♯ A B C♯ D E F♯
F♯ E D C♯ B A G♯ F♯

A
B♭/A♯
B
C
C♯/D♭
D
E♭/D♯
E
F
F♯/G♭
G
A♭/G♯

# F♯ Harmonic Minor

**Scale pattern**

F♯ G♯ A B C♯ D E♯ F♯

F♯ E♯ D C♯ B A G♯ F♯

# F♯ Melodic Minor

**Scale pattern**

F♯ G♯ A B C♯ D♯ E♯ F♯
F♯ E♮ D♮ C♯ B A G♯ F♯

A
B♭/A♯
B
C
C♯/D♭
D
E♭/D♯
E
F
F♯/G♭
G
A♭/G♯

# F♯ Dorian

**Scale pattern**

F♯ G♯ A B C♯ D♯ E F♯
F♯ E D♯ C♯ B A G♯ F♯

A
B♭/A♯
B
C
C♯/D♭
D
E♭/D♯
E
F
F♯/G♭
G
A♭/G♯

# F♯ Minor Pentatonic

| **Scale pattern** | F♯ A B C♯ E F♯<br>F♯ E C♯ B A F♯ |
|---|---|

A
B♭/A♯
B
C
C♯/D♭
D
E♭/D♯
E
F
F♯/G♭
G
A♭/G♯

# F♯ Blues

T
A
B
4 7 4 5 6 5 7

| **Scale pattern** | F♯ A B C♮ C♯ E F♯<br>F♯ E C♯ C♮ B A F♯ |
|---|---|

# F♯ Phrygian

**Scale pattern**

F♯ G A B C♯ D E F♯
F♯ E D C♯ B A G F♯

A
B♭/A♯
B
C
C♯/D♭
D
E♭/D♯
E
F
F♯/G♭
G
A♭/G♯

# F♯ Locrian

**Scale pattern**

F♯ G A B C D E F♯
F♯ E D C B A G F♯

# F♯ Half Diminished

**Scale pattern**

F♯ G♯ A B C D E F♯
F♯ E D C B A G♯ F♯

# F♯ Mixolydian

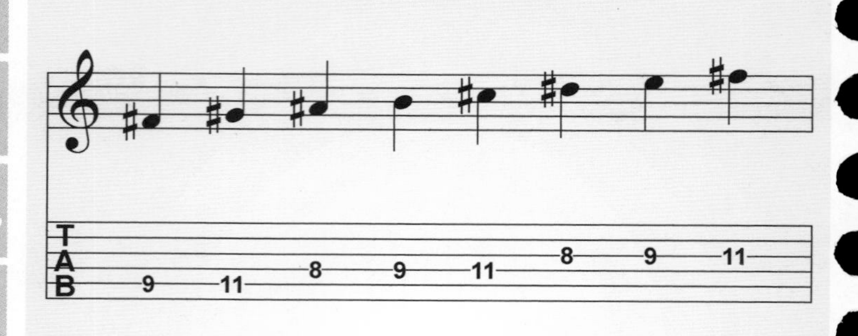

**Scale pattern**

F♯ G♯ A♯ B C♯ D♯ E F♯
F♯ E D♯ C♯ B A♯ G♯ F♯

# F♯ Phrygian Major/ Spanish Gypsy

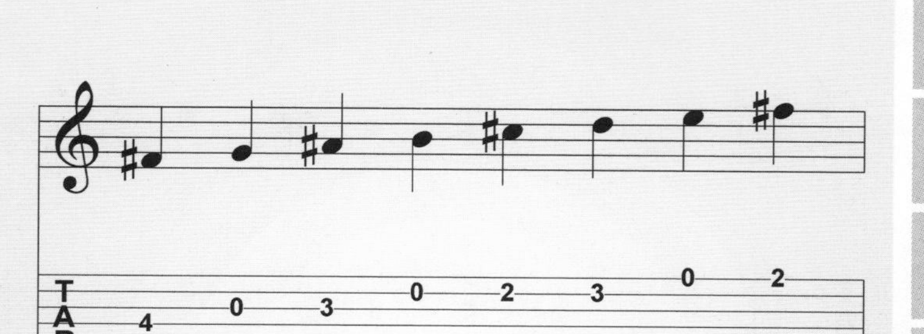

| **Scale pattern** | F♯ G A♯ B C♯ D E F♯<br>F♯ E D C♯ B A♯ G F♯ |
|---|---|

# F♯ Lydian Dominant

**Scale pattern**

F♯ G♯ A♯ B♯ C♯ D♯ E F♯

F♯ E D♯ C♯ B♯ A♯ G♯ F♯

# F♯ Diminished Wholetone/ Super Locrian/Altered

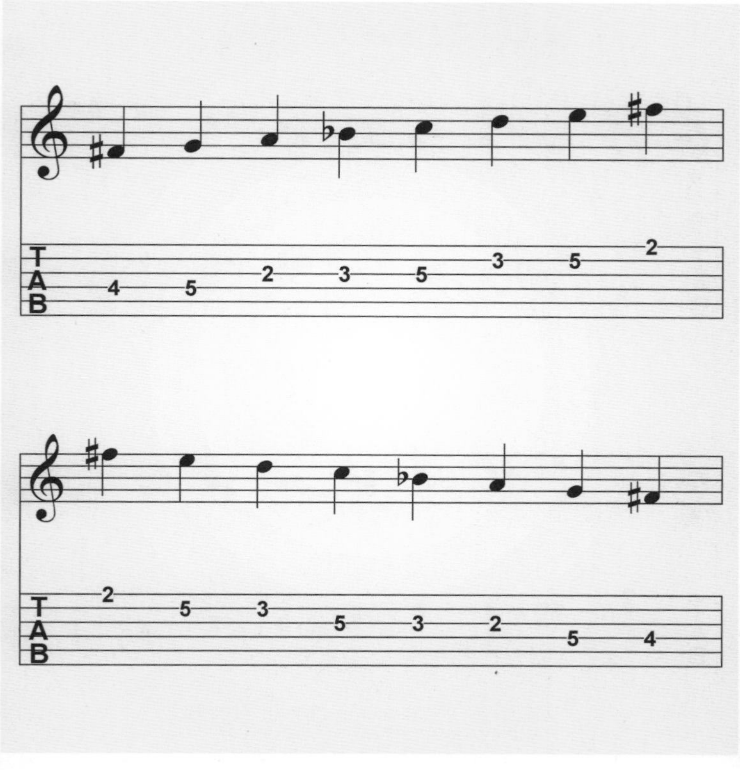

T A B: 4 5 2 3 5 3 5 2

T A B: 2 5 3 5 3 2 5 4

**Scale pattern**

F♯ G A B♭ C D E F♯
F♯ E D C B♭ A G F♯

# F♯ Diminished

**Scale pattern**

F♯ G A A♯ B♯ C♯ D♯ E F♯
F♯ E D♯ C♯ B♯ A♯ A♮ G F♯

# F♯ Chromatic

B♭/A♯
B
C
C♯/D♭
D
E♭/D♯
E
F
F♯/G♭
G
A♭/G♯

**Scale pattern** 

F♯ G G♯ A A♯ B B♯ C♯ D D♯ E E♯ F♯

F♯ E♯ E♮ D♯ D♮ C♯ B♯ B♮ A♯ A♮ G♯ G♮ F♯

A
B♭/A♯
B
C
C♯/D♭
D
E♭/D♯
E
F
F♯/G♭
G
A♭/G♯

# F♯ Wholetone

TAB
4 6 8 5 7 5 7

**Scale pattern**

F♯ G♯ A♯ C D E F♯
F♯ E D C A♯ G♯ F♯

# F♯ Neapolitan

**Scale pattern**

F♯ G A B C♯ D♯ E♯ F♯
F♯ E♯ D♯ C♯ B A G F♯

# G♭ Leading Wholetone

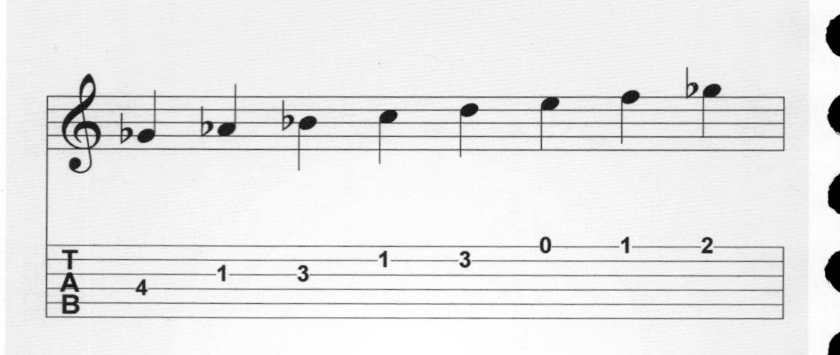

**Scale pattern**

G♭ A♭ B♭ C D E F G♭
G♭ F E D C B♭ A♭ G♭

# G♭ Lydian Augmented Dominant

| Scale pattern | G♭ A♭ B♭ C D E♭ F♭ G♭<br>G♭ F♭ E♭ D C B♭ A♭ G♭ |
|---|---|

# F♯ Lydian Dominant ♭6

| **Scale pattern** | F♯ G♯ A♯ B♯ C♯ D E F♯<br>F♯ E D C♯ B♯ A♯ G♯ F♯ |
|---|---|

B♭/A♯
B
C
C♯/D♭
D
E♭/D♯
E
F
F♯/G♭
G
A♭/G♯

# F♯ Major Locrian/Arabian

| Scale pattern | F♯ G♯ A♯ B C D E F♯<br>F♯ E D C B A♯ G♯ F♯ |
|---|---|

# F♯ Semi-Locrian ♭4

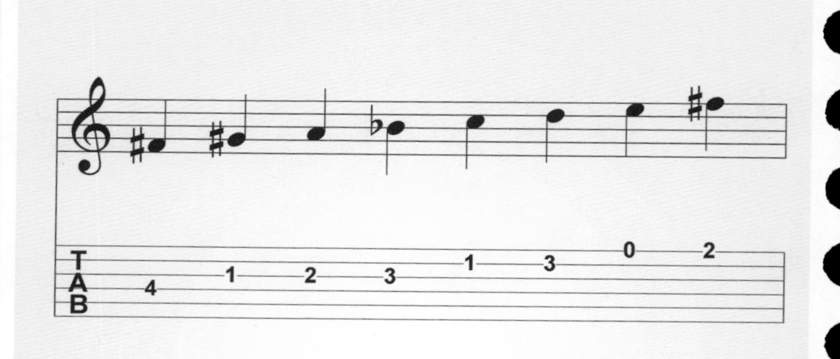

| **Scale pattern** | F♯ G♯ A B♭ C D E F♯<br>F♯ E D C B♭ A G♯ F♯ |
|---|---|

# F♯ Super-Locrian 𝄫3



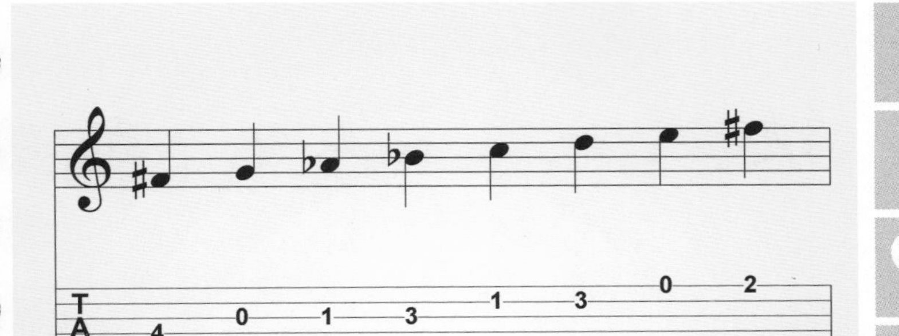

**Scale pattern**

F♯ G A♭ B♭ C D E F♯
F♯ E D C B♭ A♭ G F♯

# F♯ Bebop Dominant

| Scale pattern | F♯ G♯ A♯ B C♯ D♯ E E♯ F♯<br>F♯ E♯ E♮ D♯ C♯ B A♯ G♯ F♯ |
|---|---|

# F♯ Bebop Major

**Scale pattern**

F♯ G♯ A♯ B C♯ D♮ D♯ E♯ F♯
F♯ E♯ D♯ D♮ C♯ B A♯ G♯ F♯

# F♯ Bebop Dorian

**Scale pattern**

F♯ G♯ A A♯ B C♯ D♯ E F♯
F♯ E D♯ C♯ B A♯ A♮ G♯ F♯

# F♯ Byzantine/Arabic/ Double Harmonic Major

**Scale pattern**

F♯ G A♯ B C♯ D E♯ F♯

F♯ E♯ D C♯ B A♯ G F♯

A
B♭/A♯
B
C
C♯/D♭
D
E♭/D♯
E
F
F♯/G♭
G
A♭/G♯

# G Major

| **Scale pattern** | G A B C D E F♯ G<br>G F♯ E D C B A G |
| --- | --- |

# G Major Pentatonic

B♭/A♯
B
C
C♯/D♭
D
E♭/D♯
E
F
F♯/G♭
G
A♭/G♯


| T A B | 5 | 2 | 4 | 3 | 5 | 3 |
|---|---|---|---|---|---|---|

| T A B | 3 | 5 | 3 | 4 | 2 | 5 |
|---|---|---|---|---|---|---|

| **Scale pattern** | G A B D E G<br>G E D B A G |
|---|---|

A
B♭/A♯
B
C
C♯/D♭
D
E♭/D♯
E
F
F♯/G♭
G
A♭/G♯

# G Lydian

**Scale pattern**

G A B C♯ D E F♯ G
G F♯ E D C♯ B A G

# G Lydian Augmented

**Scale pattern**

G A B C♯ D♯ E F♯ G
G F♯ E D♯ C♯ B A G

A
B♭/A♯
B
C
C♯/D♭
D
E♭/D♯
E
F
F♯/G♭
G
A♭/G♯

A
B♭/A♯
B
C
C♯/D♭
D
E♭/D♯
E
F
F♯/G♭
G

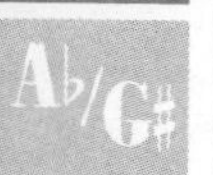


# G Natural Minor

**Scale pattern**

G A B♭ C D E♭ F G
G F E♭ D C B♭ A G

# G Harmonic Minor

TAB
5 7 8 5 7 8 7 8

TAB
8 7 8 7 5 8 7 5

**Scale pattern**

G A B♭ C D E♭ F♯ G
G F♯ E♭ D C B♭ A G

# G Melodic Minor

**Scale pattern**

G A B♭ C D E F♯ G
G F♮ E♭ D C B♭ A G

# G Dorian

**Scale pattern**

G A B♭ C D E F G
G F E D C B♭ A G

# G Minor Pentatonic

**Scale pattern**

G B♭ C D F G
G F D C B♭ G

# G Blues

**Scale pattern**

G B♭ C D♭ D♮ F G
G F D♮ D♭ C B♭ G

A
B♭/A♯
B
C
C♯/D♭
D
E♭/D♯
E
F
F♯/G♭
G
A♭/G♯

# G Phrygian

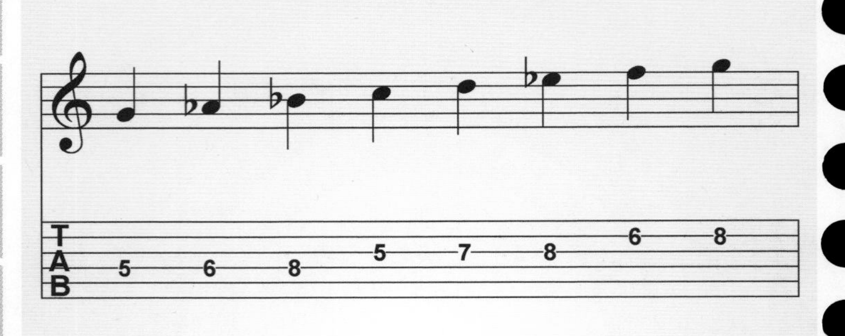

| **Scale pattern** | G A♭ B♭ C D E♭ F G<br>G F E♭ D C B♭ A♭ G |
|---|---|

# G Locrian

T A B: 5 6 8 5 6 8 6 8

T A B: 8 6 8 6 5 8 6 5

**Scale pattern**

G A♭ B♭ C D♭ E♭ F G
G F E♭ D♭ C B♭ A♭ G

# G Half Diminished

**Scale pattern**

G A B♭ C D♭ E♭ F G
G F E♭ D♭ C B♭ A G

# G Mixolydian

| Scale pattern | G A B C D E F G<br>G F E D C B A G |
|---|---|

A
B♭/A#
B
C
C#/D♭
D
E♭/D#
E
F
F#/G♭
G
A♭/G#

# G Phrygian Major/ Spanish Gypsy

**Scale pattern**

G A♭ B C D E♭ F G
G F E♭ D C B A♭ G

# G Lydian Dominant

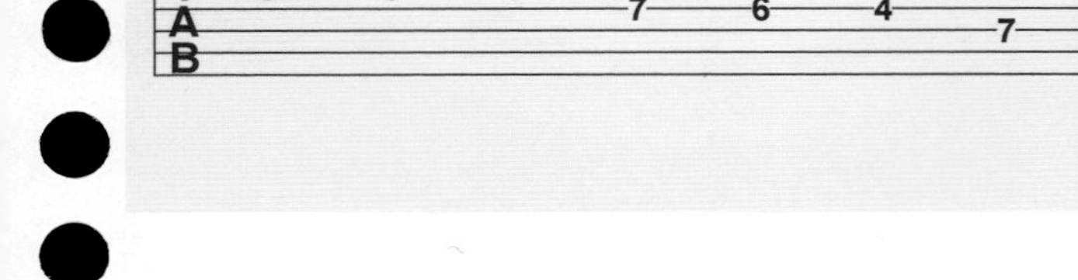


**Scale pattern**

G A B C♯ D E F G
G F E D C♯ B A G

# G Diminished Wholetone/ Super Locrian/Altered

**Scale pattern**

G A♭ B♭ C♭ D♭ E♭ F G
G F E♭ D♭ C♭ B♭ A♭ G

# G Diminished

| **Scale pattern** | G A♭ B♭ B♮ C♯ D E F G<br>G F E D C♯ B♮ B♭ A♭ G |
|---|---|

A
B♭/A♯
B
C
C♯/D♭
D
E♭/D♯
E
F
F♯/G♭
G
A♭/G♯

# G Chromatic

**Scale pattern**

G A♭ A♮ B♭ B♮ C C♯ D E♭ E♮ F F♯ G

G F♯ F♮ E E♭ D C♯ C♮ B B♭ A A♭ G

# G Wholetone

**Scale pattern**

G A B C♯ D♯ F G
G F D♯ C♯ B A G

# G Neapolitan

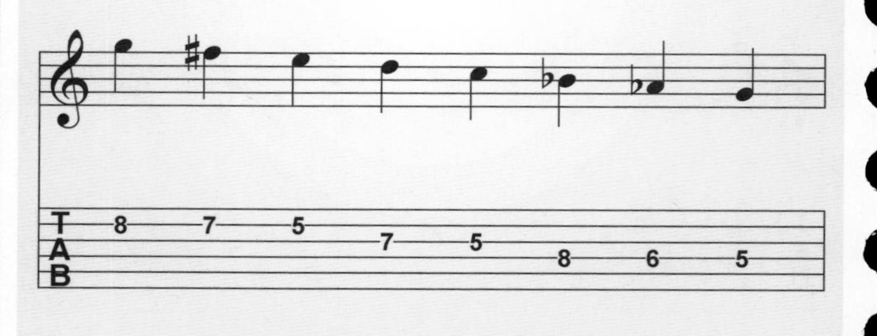


**Scale pattern**

G A♭ B♭ C D E F♯ G
G F♯ E D C B♭ A♭ G

# G Leading Wholetone

| **Scale pattern** | G A B C♯ D♯ E♯ F♯ G<br>G F♯ E♯ D♯ C♯ B A G |
|---|---|

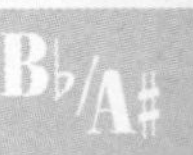

A

B♭/A♯
B
C
C♯/D♭
D
E♭/D♯
E
F
F♯/G♭
G
A♭/G♯

# G Lydian Augmented Dominant

**Scale pattern**

G A B C♯ D♯ E F G
G F E D♯ C♯ B A G

# G Lydian Dominant ♭6

| **Scale pattern** | G A B C♯ D E♭ F G<br>G F E♭ D C♯ B A G |
|---|---|


A
B♭/A♯
B
C
C♯/D♭
D
E♭/D♯
E
F
F♯/G♭
G
A♭/G♯

# G Major Locrian/Arabian

| **Scale pattern** | G A B C D♭ E♭ F G<br>G F E♭ D♭ C B A G |
|---|---|

# G Semi-Locrian ♭4

A
B♭/A♯
B
C
C♯/D♭
D
E♭/D♯
E
F
F♯/G♭
G
A♭/G♯

**Scale pattern**

G A B♭ C♭ D♭ E♭ F G
G F E♭ D♭ C♭ B♭ A G

# G Super-Locrian 𝄫3

**Scale pattern**

G G♯ A B C♯ D♯ F G
G F D♯ C♯ B A A♭ G

# G Bebop Dominant

| Scale pattern | G A B C D E F F♯ G<br>G F♯ F♮ E D C B A G |
|---|---|

A
B♭/A♯
B
C
C♯/D♭
D
E♭/D♯
E
F
F♯/G♭
G
A♭/G♯

# G Bebop Major

**Scale pattern**

G A B C D E♭ E♮ F♯ G
G F♯ E♮ E♭ D C B A G

# G Bebop Dorian

**Scale pattern**

G A B♭ B♮ C D E F G
G F E D C B B♭ A G

A
B♭/A♯
B
C
C♯/D♭
D
E♭/D♯
E
F
F♯/G♭
G
A♭/G♯

# G Byzantine/Arabic/ Double Harmonic Major

**Scale pattern**

G A♭ B C D E♭ F♯ G

G F♯ E♭ D C B A♭ G

# A♭ Major

| **Scale pattern** | A♭ B♭ C D♭ E♭ F G A♭<br>A♭ G F E♭ D♭ C B♭ A♭ |
|---|---|

# A♭ Major Pentatonic

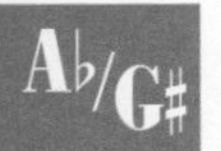


**Scale pattern**

A♭ B♭ C E♭ F A♭
A♭ F E♭ C B♭ A♭

# A♭ Lydian

**Scale pattern**

A♭ B♭ C D E♭ F G A♭
A♭ G F E♭ D C B♭ A♭

# A♭ Lydian Augmented

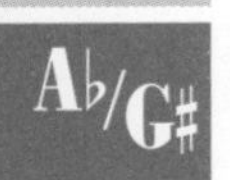



**Scale pattern**

A♭ B♭ C D E F G A♭
A♭ G F E D C B♭ A♭

# G♯ Natural Minor

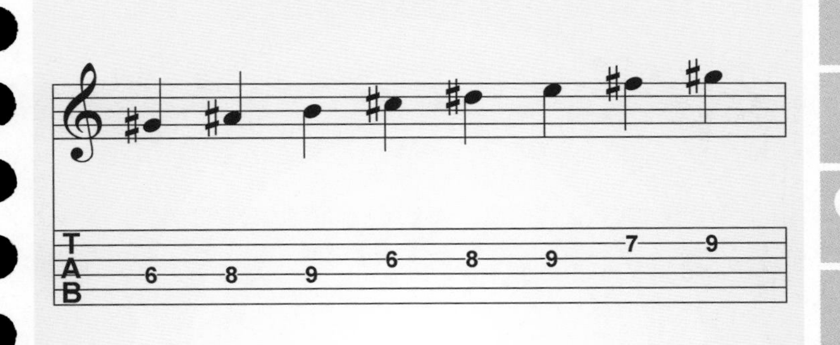

| **Scale pattern** | G♯ A♯ B C♯ D♯ E F♯ G♯<br>G♯ F♯ E D♯ C♯ B A♯ G♯ |
|---|---|

# G♯ Harmonic Minor

**Scale pattern**

G♯ A♯ B C♯ D♯ E F× G♯
G♯ F× E D♯ C♯ B A♯ G♯

# G♯ Melodic Minor

| **Scale pattern** | G♯ A♯ B C♯ D♯ E♯ F𝄪 G♯<br>G♯ F♯ E♮ D♯ C♯ B A♯ G♯ |
|---|---|

# G♯ Dorian

**Scale pattern**

G♯ A♯ B C♯ D♯ E♯ F♯ G♯
G♯ F♯ E♯ D♯ C♯ B A♯ G♯

# G♯ Minor Pentatonic

**Scale pattern**

G♯ B C♯ D♯ F♯ G♯
G♯ F♯ D♯ C♯ B G♯

A
B♭/A♯
B
C
C♯/D♭
D
E♭/D♯
E
F
F♯/G♭
G
A♭/G♯

# G♯ Blues

**Scale pattern**

G♯ B C♯ D♮ D♯ F♯ G♯
G♯ F♯ D♯ D♮ C♯ B G♯

# G♯ Phrygian

**Scale pattern**

G♯ A B C♯ D♯ E F♯ G♯
G♯ F♯ E D♯ C♯ B A G♯

# G♯ Locrian

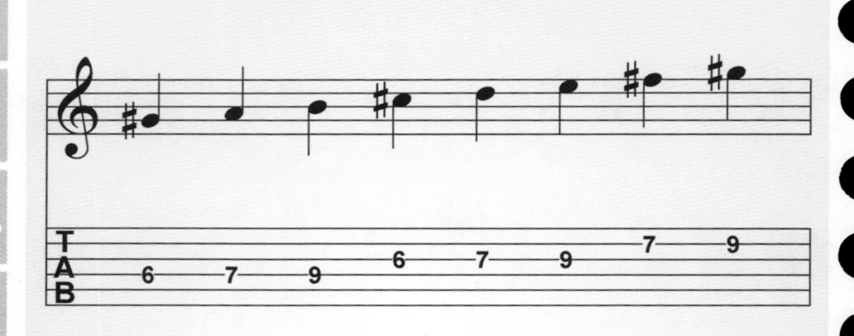

**Scale pattern**

G♯ A B C♯ D E F♯ G♯
G♯ F♯ E D C♯ B A G♯

# G♯ Half Diminished

B♭/A♯
B
C
C♯/D♭
D
E♭/D♯
E
F
F♯/G♭
G
A♭/G♯

| **Scale pattern** | G♯ A♯ B C♯ D E F♯ G♯<br>G♯ F♯ E D C♯ B A♯ G♯ |
|---|---|

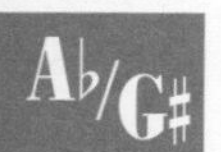


# A♭ Mixolydian

**Scale pattern**

A♭ B♭ C D♭ E♭ F G♭ A♭
A♭ G♭ F E♭ D♭ C B♭ A♭

# G♯ Phrygian Major/ Spanish Gypsy

**Scale pattern**

G♯ A B♯ C♯ D♯ E F♯ G♯
G♯ F♯ E D♯ C♯ B♯ A G♯

A
B♭/A♯
B
C
C♯/D♭
D
E♭/D♯
E
F
F♯/G♭
G

# A♭ Lydian Dominant

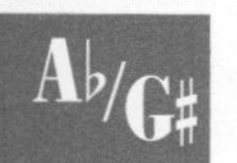


**Scale pattern**

A♭ B♭ C D E♭ F G♭ A♭
A♭ G♭ F E♭ D C B♭ A♭

# G♯ Diminished Wholetone/ Super Locrian/Altered

T
A
B
6 7 4 5 7 5 7 4

T
A
B
4 7 5 7 5 4 7 6

| Scale pattern | G♯ A B C D E F♯ G♯ |
| --- | --- |
| | G♯ F♯ E D C B A G♯ |

# G♯ Diminished

**Scale pattern**

G♯ A B C D D♯ E♯ F♯ G♯
G♯ F♯ E♯ D♯ D♮ C B A G♯

# G♯ Chromatic

**Scale pattern** G♯ A A♯ B B♯ C♯ C× D♯ E E♯ F♯ F× G♯
G♯ F× F♯ E♯ E♮ D♯ C× C♯ B♯ B♮ A♯ A♮ G♯

A
B♭/A♯
B
C
C♯/D♭
D
E♭/D♯
E
F
F♯/G♭
G

# A♭ Wholetone

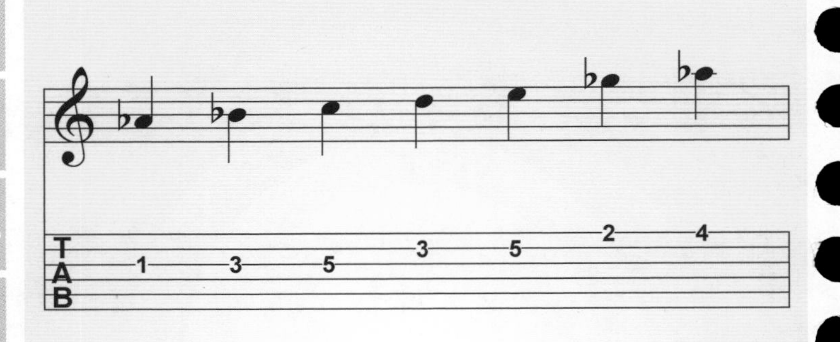

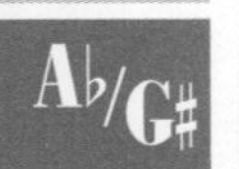


**Scale pattern**

A♭ B♭ C D E G♭ A♭
A♭ G♭ E D C B♭ A♭

# G♯ Neapolitan

**Scale pattern**

G♯ A B C♯ D♯ E♯ F𝄪 G♯
G♯ F𝄪 E♯ D♯ C♯ B A G♯

# A♭ Leading Wholetone

**Scale pattern**

A♭ B♭ C D E F♯ G A♭
A♭ G F♯ E D C B♭ A♭

# A♭ Lydian Augmented Dominant

**Scale pattern**

A♭ B♭ C D E F G♭ A♭
A♭ G♭ F E D C B♭ A♭

# A♭ Lydian Dominant ♭6

**Scale pattern**

A♭ B♭ C D E♭ F♭ G♭ A♭
A♭ G♭ F♭ E♭ D C B♭ A♭

# G♯ Major Locrian/Arabian

**Scale pattern**

G♯ A♯ B♯ C♯ D E F♯ G♯
G♯ F♯ E D C♯ B♯ A♯ G♯

# G♯ Semi-Locrian ♭4

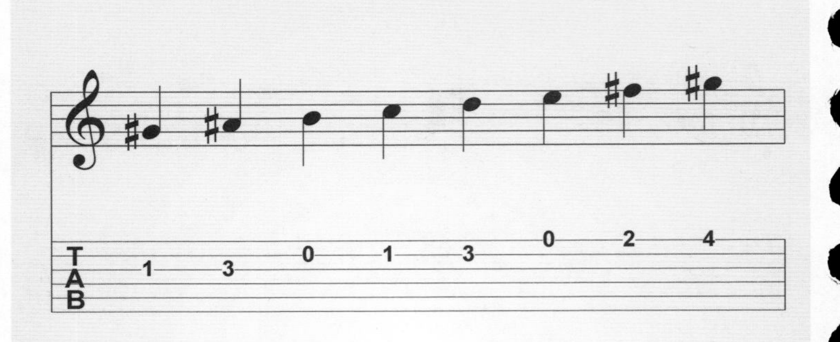

**Scale pattern**

G♯ A♯ B C D E F♯ G♯
G♯ F♯ E D C B A♯ G♯

# G♯ Super-Locrian 𝄫3

| **Scale pattern** | G♯ A B♭ C D E F♯ G♯<br>G♯ F♯ E D C B♭ A G♯ |
|---|---|

A
B♭/A♯
B
C
C♯/D♭
D
E♭/D♯
E
F
F♯/G♭
G
A♭/G♯

# A♭ Bebop Dominant

**Scale pattern**

A♭ B♭ C D♭ E♭ F G♭ G♮ A♭
A♭ G G♭ F E♭ D♭ C B♭ A♭

# A♭ Bebop Major

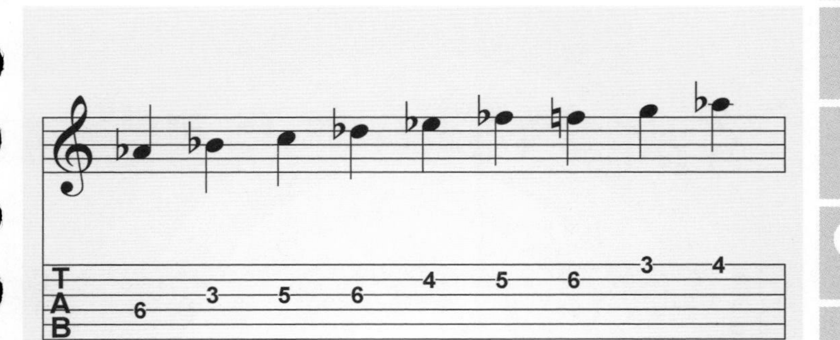

**Scale pattern**

A♭ B♭ C D♭ E♭ F♭ F♮ G A♭
A♭ G F♮ F♭ E♭ D♭ C B♭ A♭

A
B♭/A♯
B
C
C♯/D♭
D
E♭/D♯
E
F
F♯/G♭
G
A♭/G♯

# G♯ Bebop Dorian

**Scale pattern**

G♯ A♯ B B♯ C♯ D♯ E♯ F♯ G♯
G♯ F♯ E♯ D♯ C♯ B♯ B♮ A♯ G♯

A
B♭/A♯
B
C
C♯/D♭
D
E♭/D♯
E
F
F♯/G♭
G

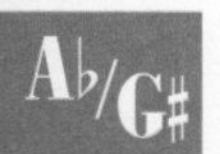